His Life
A Complete Story in the
Words of the Four Gospels

William E. Barton

Theodore G. Soares

Sydney Strong

Contents

HIS LIFE
A COMPLETE STORY IN THE
WORDS OF THE
FOUR GOSPELS

BY

William E. Barton, Theodore G. Soares,
Sydney Strong

PREFACE.

The four Gospels, each telling in its own way the story of the Life of Jesus, are the rich heritage of Christians. No one of the Gospels could be spared. But in reading any one of the four we miss some of the familiar words and incidents we love. Almost from the days of the Apostles there have been attempts to unite the Gospels in a single narrative. The first of these efforts, so far as we know, was undertaken by the devout scholar Tatian, soon after 173 A.D. His book served a useful purpose in his own and later generations, and is now a valuable witness to the antiquity and early acceptance of our four Gospels. There have been many harmonies of the Gospel from the second century to the present; and they are all but indispensable to the scholar. Almost every minister keeps one at his elbow. But these, for the most part, are made for purposes of scholarly comparison, and not for general reading. Moreover, they are expensive.

The editors of this little book have undertaken to prepare an interwoven story of the Life of Jesus from the four Gospels for popular reading. A booklet that may be carried in the pocket, and may be sold, in paper binding, for ten cents, has been their ambition. They have been led to this undertaking by the large demand for copies of their booklet, "HIS LAST WEEK," which comprises the last third of this volume, whose use at Easter time has brought them many requests for the complete Gospel story, interwoven in the same manner.

The work of preparation has been done by three ministers of Oak Park, in suburban Chicago, who have shared equally the labor, but the undertaking has the support and co-operation of the entire group of fifteen local pastors, representing six different denominations. To this larger group of brethren is due a grateful acknowledgment of sympathy and assistance. The book has at least the value of an illustration in practical interdenominational co-operation. In the spirit of this fine

fellowship it is commended to Christians of every name.
THE EDITORS

=HIS BIRTH AND BOYHOOD=

THE DIVINE ANNOUNCINGS
THE WORD MADE FLESH.

In the beginning was the Word, and the Word was with God, and the Word was God. The same was in the beginning with God. All things were made through him; and without him was not anything made that hath been made. In him was life; and the life was the light of men. And the light shineth in the darkness; and the darkness apprehended it not.

There came a man, sent from God, whose name was John. The same came for witness, that he might bear witness of the light, that all might believe through him. He was not the light, but came that he might bear witness of the light. There was the true light, even the light which lighteth every man, coming into the world. He was in the world, and the world was made through him, and the world knew him not. He came unto his own, and they that were his own received him not. But as many as received him, to them gave he the right to become children of God, even to them that believe on his name: who were born, not of blood, nor of the will of the flesh, nor of the will of man, but of God.

And the Word became flesh, and dwelt among us (and we beheld his glory, glory as of the only begotten from the Father), full of grace and truth. John beareth witness of him, and crieth, saying, "This was he of whom I said, He that cometh after me is become before me: for he was before me."

For of his fulness we all received, and grace for grace. For the law was given through Moses; grace and truth came through Jesus Christ. No man hath seen God at any time; the only begotten Son, who is in the bosom of the Father, he hath declared him.

THE PROMISED BIRTH OF JOHN THE BAPTIST.

There was in the days of Herod, king of Judaea, a certain priest named Zacharias, of the course of Abijah: and he had a wife of the daughters of Aaron, and her name was Elisabeth. And they were both righteous before God, walking in all the commandments and ordinances of the Lord blameless. And they had no child, because that Elisabeth was barren, and they both were now well stricken in years.

Now it came to pass, while he executed the priest's office before God in the order of his course, according to the custom of the priest's office, his lot was to enter into the temple of the Lord and burn incense. And the whole multitude of the people were praying without at the hour of incense.

And there appeared unto him an angel of the Lord standing on the right side of the altar of incense.

And Zacharias was troubled when he saw him, and fear fell upon him. But the angel said unto him, "Fear not, Zacharias: because thy supplication is heard, and thy wife Elisabeth shall bear thee a son, and thou shalt call his name John. And thou shalt have joy and gladness; and many shall rejoice at his birth. For he shall be great in the sight of the Lord, and he shall drink no wine nor strong drink; and he shall be filled with the Holy Spirit, even from his mother's womb. And many of the children of Israel shall he turn unto the Lord their God. And he shall go before his face in the spirit and power of Elijah, to turn the hearts of the fathers to the children, and the disobedient to walk in the wisdom of the just; to make ready for the Lord a people prepared for him."

And Zacharias said unto the angel, "Whereby shall I know this? for I am an old man, and my wife well stricken in years."

And the angel answering said unto him, "I am Gabriel, that stand in the presence of God; and I was sent to speak unto thee, and to bring thee these good tidings. And behold, thou shalt be silent and not able to speak, until the day that these things shall come to pass, because thou believedst not my words, which shall be fulfilled in their season."

And the people were waiting for Zacharias, and they marvelled while he tarried in the temple. And when he came out, he could not speak unto them: and they perceived that he had seen a vision in the temple: and he continued making signs unto them, and remained dumb.

And it came to pass, when the days of his ministration were fulfilled, he departed unto his house.

And after these days Elisabeth his wife conceived; and she hid herself five months, saying, "Thus hath the Lord done unto me in the days wherein he looked upon me, to take away my reproach among men."

THE ANGEL'S VISIT TO MARY.

Now in the sixth month the angel Gabriel was sent from God unto a city of Galilee, named Nazareth, to a virgin betrothed to a man whose name was Joseph, of the house of David; and the virgin's name was Mary. And he came in unto her, and said, "Hail, thou that art highly favored, the Lord is with thee."

But she was greatly troubled at the saying, and cast in her mind what manner of salutation this might be.

And the angel said unto her, "Fear not, Mary: for thou hast found favor with God And behold, thou shalt conceive in thy womb, and bring forth a son, and shalt call his name JESUS. He shall be great, and shall be called the Son of the Most High: and the Lord God shall give unto him the throne of his father David: and he shall reign over the house of Jacob forever; and of his kingdom there shall be no end."

And Mary said unto the angel, "How shall this be, seeing I know not a man?"

And the angel answered and said unto her, "The Holy Spirit shall come upon thee, and the power of the Most High shall overshadow thee: wherefore also the holy thing which is begotten shall be called the Son of God. And behold, Elisabeth thy kinswoman, she also hath conceived a son in her old age; and this is the sixth month with her that was called barren. For no word from God shall be void of power."

And Mary said, "Behold, the handmaid of the Lord; be it unto me according to thy word"

And the angel departed from her.

MARY'S VISIT TO HER COUSIN.

And Mary arose in these days and went into the hill country with haste, into a city of Judah; and entered into the house of Zacharias and saluted Elisabeth. And it came to pass, when Elisabeth heard the salutation of Mary, the babe leaped in her womb; and Elisabeth was filled with the Holy Spirit; and she lifted up her voice with a loud cry, and said, "Blessed art thou among women, and blessed is the fruit of thy womb. And whence is this to me, that the mother of my Lord should come unto me? For behold, when the voice of thy salutation came into mine ears, the babe leaped in my womb for joy. And blessed is she that believed; for there shall be a fulfilment of the things which have been spoken to her from the Lord."

MARY'S SONG.

And Mary said,

"My soul doth magnify the Lord.
And my spirit hath rejoiced in God my Saviour.
For he hath looked upon the low estate of his handmaid:
For behold, from henceforth all generations shall call me blessed.
For he that is mighty hath done to me great things;
And holy is his name.
And his mercy is unto generations and generations
On them that fear him.
He hath showed strength with his arm:
He hath scattered the proud in the imagination of their heart.
He hath put down princes from their thrones,
And hath exalted them of low degree.
The hungry he hath filled with good things;

And the rich he hath sent empty away.
He hath given help to Israel his servant,
That he might remember mercy
(As he spake unto our fathers)
Toward Abraham and his seed for ever."

And Mary abode with her about three months, and returned unto her house.

THE BIRTH OF JOHN THE BAPTIST.

Now Elisabeth's time was fulfilled that she should be delivered; and she brought forth a son. And her neighbors and her kinsfolk heard that the Lord had magnified his mercy towards her; and they rejoiced with her.

And it came to pass on the eighth day, that they came to circumcise the child; and they would have called him Zacharias, after the name of his father.

And his mother answered and said, "Not so; but he shall be called John."

And they said unto her, "There is none of thy kindred that is called by this name."

And they made signs to his father, what he would have him called.

And he asked for a writing tablet, and wrote, saying, "His name is John."

And they marvelled all. And his mouth was opened immediately, and his tongue loosed, and he spake, blessing God.

And fear came on all that dwelt round about them: and all these sayings were noised abroad throughout all the hill country of Judaea.

And all that heard them laid them up in their heart, saying, "What then shall this child be?"

For the hand of the Lord was with him.

THE SONG OF ZACHARIAS.

And his father Zacharias was filled with the Holy Spirit, and prophesied, saying,

> "Blessed be the Lord the God of Israel;
> For he hath visited and wrought redemption for his people,
> And hath raised up a horn of salvation for us
> In the house of his servant David
> (As he spake by the mouth of his holy prophets that have been
>   from of old),
> Salvation from our enemies and from the hand of all that hate us;
> To show mercy towards our fathers.
> And to remember his holy covenant;
> The oath which he sware unto Abraham our father,
> To grant unto us that we being delivered out of the hand of
>   our enemies
> Should serve him without fear,
> In holiness and righteousness before him all our days.
> Yea and thou, child, shalt be called the prophet of the Most High:
> For thou shalt go before the face of the Lord to make ready
>   his ways;
> To give knowledge of salvation unto his people
> In the remission of their sins,
> Because of the tender mercy of our God,
> Whereby the dayspring from on high shall visit us,
> To shine upon them that sit in darkness and the shadow of death;
> To guide our feet into the way of peace."

And the child grew, and waxed strong in spirit, and was in the deserts till the day of his showing unto Israel.

THE BIRTH AND INFANCY OF JESUS JOSEPH AND MARY.

Now the birth of Jesus Christ was on this wise: When his mother Mary had been betrothed to Joseph, before they came together she was found with child of the Holy Spirit. And Joseph her husband, being a righteous man, and not willing to make her a public example, was minded to put her away privily.

But when he thought on these things, behold, an angel of the Lord appeared unto him in a dream, saying, "Joseph, thou son of David, fear not to take unto thee Mary thy wife: for that which is conceived in her is of the Holy Spirit. And she shall bring forth a son; and thou shalt call his name JESUS; for it is he that shall save his people from their sins."

Now all this is come to pass, that it might be fulfilled which was spoken by the Lord through the prophet, saying,

"Behold, the virgin shall be with child, and shall bring
forth a son,
And they shall call his name Immanuel;"

which is, being interpreted, "God with us."

And Joseph arose from his sleep, and did as the angel of the Lord commanded him, and took unto him his wife; and knew her not till she had brought forth a son.

THE BIRTH OF JESUS.

Now it came to pass in those days, there went out a decree from Caesar Augustus, that all the world should be enrolled. This was the first enrolment made when Quirinius was governor of Syria. And all went to enrol themselves, every one to his own city. And Joseph also went up from Galilee, out of the city of Nazareth, into

Judaea, to the city of David, which is called Bethlehem, because he was of the house and family of David; to enrol himself with Mary, who was betrothed to him, being great with child.

And it came to pass, while they were there, the days were fulfilled that she should be delivered. And she brought forth her firstborn son; and she wrapped him in swaddling clothes, and laid him in a manger, because there was no room for them in the inn.

THE ANGELS AND THE SHEPHERDS.

And there were shepherds in the same country abiding in the field, and keeping watch by night over their flock. And an angel of the Lord stood by them, and the glory of the Lord shone round about them: and they were sore afraid.

And the angel said unto them, "Be not afraid; for behold, I bring you good tidings of great joy which shall be to all the people: for there is born to you this day in the city of David a Saviour, who is Christ the Lord. And this is the sign unto you: Ye shall find a babe wrapped in swaddling clothes, and lying in a manger."

And suddenly there was with the angel a multitude of the heavenly host praising God, and saying,

"Glory to God in the highest,   And on earth peace among men in whom he is well pleased."

And it came to pass, when the angels went away from them into heaven, the shepherds said one to another, "Let us now go even unto Bethlehem, and see this thing that is come to pass, which the Lord hath made known unto us."

And they came with haste, and found both Mary and Joseph, and the babe lying in the manger. And when they saw it, they made known concerning the saying which was spoken to them about this child.

And all that heard it wondered at the things which were spoken unto them by the shepherds.

But Mary kept all these sayings, pondering them in her heart.

And the shepherds returned, glorifying and praising God for all the things that they had heard and seen, even as it was spoken unto them.

THE CIRCUMCISION.

And when eight days were fulfilled for circumcising him, his name was called JESUS, which was so called by the angel before he was conceived in the womb.

THE PRESENTATION IN THE TEMPLE.

And when the days of their purification according to the law of Moses were fulfilled, they brought him up to Jerusalem to present him to the Lord (as it is written in the law of the Lord, Every male that openeth the womb shall be called holy to the Lord), and to offer a sacrifice according to that which is said in the law of the Lord, "A pair of turtledoves, or two young pigeons."

And behold, there was a man in Jerusalem, whose name was Simeon: and this man was righteous and devout, looking for the consolation of Israel: and the Holy Spirit was upon him. And it had been revealed unto him by the Holy Spirit, that he should not see death, before he had seen the Lord's Christ. And he came in the Spirit into the temple: and when the parents brought in the child Jesus, that they might do concerning him after the custom of the law, then he received him into his arms, and blessed God, and said,

"Now, lettest thou thy servant depart, Lord,
According to thy word, in peace;
For mine eyes have seen thy salvation,
Which thou hast prepared before the face of all peoples;
A light for revelation to the Gentiles,
And the glory of thy people Israel."

And his father and his mother were marvelling at the things which were spoken concerning him; and Simeon blessed them, and said unto Mary his mother,

"Behold, this child is set for the falling and the rising of
    many in Israel;
And for a sign which is spoken against;
Yea and a sword shall pierce through thine own soul;
That thoughts out of many hearts may be revealed."

And there was one Anna, a prophetess, the daughter of Phanuel, of the tribe of Asher (she was of a great age, having lived with a husband seven years from her virginity, and she had been a widow even unto fourscore and four years), who departed not from the temple, worshipping with fastings and supplications night and day. And coming up at that very hour she gave thanks unto God, and spake of him to all them that were looking for the redemption of Jerusalem.

THE VISIT OF THE WISE MEN.

Now when Jesus was born in Bethlehem of Judaea in the days of Herod the king, behold, Wise-men from the east came to Jerusalem, saying, "Where is he that is born King of the Jews? for we saw his star in the east, and are come to worship him."

And when Herod the king heard it, he was troubled, and all Jerusalem with him. And gathering together all the chief priests and scribes of the people, he inquired of them where the Christ should be born. And they said unto him, "In Bethlehem of Judaea: for thus it is written through the prophet,

"'And thou Bethlehem, land of Judah,
Art in no wise least among the princes of Judah:
For out of thee shall come forth a governor,
Who shall be shepherd of my people Israel.'"

Then Herod privily called the Wise-men, and learned of them exactly what time the star appeared. And he sent them to Bethlehem, and said, "Go and search out exactly concerning the young child; and when ye have found him, bring me word, that I also may come and worship him."

And they, having heard the king, went their way; and lo, the star, which they saw in the east, went before them, till it came and stood over where the young child was. And when they saw the star, they rejoiced with exceeding great joy. And they came into the house and saw the young child with Mary his mother; and they fell down and worshipped him; and opening their treasures they offered unto him gifts, gold and frankincense and myrrh.

And being warned of God in a dream that they should not return to Herod, they departed into their own country another way.

THE FLIGHT INTO EGYPT.

Now when they were departed, behold, an angel of the Lord appeareth to Joseph in a dream, saying, "Arise and take the young child and his mother, and flee into Egypt, and be thou there until I tell thee: for Herod will seek the young child to destroy him." He arose and took the young child and his mother by night, and departed into Egypt; and was there until the death of Herod: that it might be fulfilled which was spoken by the Lord through the prophet, saying, "Out of Egypt did I call my son."

Then Herod, when he saw that he was mocked of the Wise-men, was exceeding wroth, and sent forth, and slew all the male children that were in Bethlehem, and in all the borders thereof, from two years old and under, according to the time which he had exactly learned of the Wise-men. Then was fulfilled that which was spoken through Jeremiah the prophet, saying,

"A voice was heard in Ramah,
Weeping and great mourning,
Rachel weeping for her children;
And she would not be comforted, because they are not."

THE LIFE IN NAZARETH
THE RETURN TO NAZARETH.

But when Herod was dead, behold, an angel of the Lord appeareth in a dream to Joseph in Egypt, saying, "Arise and take the young child and his mother, and go into the land of Israel: for they are dead that sought the young child's life."

And he arose and took the young child and his mother, and came into the land of Israel.

But when he heard that Archelaus was reigning over Judaea in the room of his father Herod, he was afraid to go thither: and being warned of God in a dream, he withdrew into the parts of Galilee, and came and dwelt in their own city Nazareth; that it might be fulfilled which was spoken through the prophets, that he should be called a Nazarene.

And the child grew, and waxed strong, filled with wisdom: and the grace of God was upon him.

THE BOYHOOD VISIT TO JERUSALEM.

And his parents went every year to Jerusalem at the feast of the passover. And when he was twelve years old, they went up after the custom of the feast; and when they had fulfilled the days, as they were returning, the boy Jesus tarried behind in Jerusalem; and his parents knew it not; but supposing him to be in the company, they went a day's journey: and they sought for him among their kinsfolk and acquaintance: and when they found him not, they returned to Jerusalem, seeking for him.

And it came to pass, after three days they found him in the temple, sitting in the midst of the teachers, both hearing them, and asking them questions: and all that heard him were amazed at his understanding and his answers.

And when they saw him, they were astonished; and his mother said unto him, "Son, why hast thou thus dealt with us? behold, thy father and I sought thee sorrowing."

And he said unto them, "How is it that ye sought me? knew ye not that I must be in my Father's house?"

And they understood not the saying which he spake unto them.

THE EIGHTEEN SILENT YEARS.

And he went down with them, and came to Nazareth; and he was subject unto them: and his mother kept all these sayings in her heart.

And Jesus advanced in wisdom and stature, and in favor with God and men.

=THE BEGINNINGS OF HIS MINISTRY=

JESUS AND JOHN THE BAPTIST
THE VOICE IN THE WILDERNESS.

Now in the fifteenth year of the reign of Tiberius Caesar, Pontius Pilate being governor of Judaea, and Herod being tetrarch of Galilee, and his brother Philip tetrarch of the region of Ituraea and Trachonitis, and Lysanias tetrarch of Abilene, in the high-priesthood of Annas and Caiaphas, the word of God came unto John the son of Zacharias in the wilderness.

And John was clothed with camel's hair, and had a leathern girdle about his loins, and did eat locusts and wild honey.

And he came into all the region round about the Jordan, preaching the baptism of repentance unto remission of sins; and saying, "Repent ye; for the kingdom of heaven is at hand."

For this is he that was spoken of by Isaiah the prophet, saying,

"The voice of one crying in the wilderness,
Make ye ready the way of the Lord,
Make his paths straight.
Every valley shall be filled,
And every mountain and hill shall be brought low;
And the crooked shall become straight,
And the rough ways smooth;
And all flesh shall see the salvation of God."

And there went out to him all the country of Judaea, and all they of Jerusalem, and they were baptized of him in the river Jordan, confessing their sins.

But when he saw many of the Pharisees and Sadducees coming to his baptism he said unto them, "Ye offspring of vipers, who warned you to flee from the wrath to come? Bring forth therefore fruits worthy of repentance, and begin not to say within yourselves, 'We have Abraham to our father': for I say unto you, that God is able of these stones to raise up children unto Abraham. And even now the axe also lieth at the root of the trees: every tree therefore that bringeth not forth good fruit is hewn down, and cast into the fire."

And the multitudes asked him, saying, "What then must we do?"

And he answered and said unto them, "He that hath two coats, let him impart to him that hath none; and he that hath food, let him do likewise."

And there came also publicans to be baptized, and they said unto him, "Teacher, what must we do?"

And he said unto them, "Extort no more than that which is appointed you."

And soldiers also asked him, saying, "And we, what must we do?"

And he said unto them, "Extort from no man by violence, neither accuse any one wrongfully; and be content with your wages."

And as the people were in expectation, and all men reasoned in their hearts concerning John, whether haply he were the Christ; John answered, saying unto them all, "I indeed baptize you with water; but there cometh he that is mightier than I, the latchet of whose shoes I am not worthy to unloose: he shall baptize you in the Holy Spirit and in fire: whose fan is in his hand, thoroughly to cleanse his threshing-floor, and to gather the wheat into his garner; but the chaff he will burn up with unquenchable fire."

With many other exhortations therefore preached he good tidings unto the people.

THE BAPTISM OF JESUS.

And it came to pass in those days, when all the people were baptized, that Jesus came from Nazareth of Galilee to the Jordan unto John, to be baptized of him.

But John would have hindered him, saying, "I have need to be baptized of thee, and comest thou to me?"

But Jesus answering said unto him, "Suffer it now: for thus it becometh us to fulfil all righteousness."

Then he suffereth him. And Jesus, when he was baptized, went up straightway from the water; and lo, the heavens were opened unto him, and he saw the Spirit of God descending as a dove, and coming upon him; and lo, a voice out of the heavens, saying, "This is my beloved Son, in whom I am well pleased."

THE TEMPTATION IN THE WILDERNESS.

Then straightway was Jesus led up of the Spirit into the wilderness to be tempted of the devil, and he was with the wild beasts, and did eat nothing in those days. And when he had fasted forty days and forty nights, he afterward hungered.

And the tempter came and said unto him, "If thou art the Son of God, command that these stones become bread."

But he answered and said, "It is written, 'Man shall not live by bread alone, but by every word that proceedeth out of the mouth of God.'"

Then the devil taketh him into the holy city; and he set him on the pinnacle of the temple, and saith unto him, "If thou art the Son of God, cast thyself down: for it is written,

"'He shall give his angels charge concerning thee, to guard thee.'

and,

"'On their hands they shall bear thee up,
Lest haply thou dash thy foot against a stone.'"

Jesus said unto him, "Again it is written, 'Thou shalt not make trial of the Lord thy God.'"

Again, the devil taketh him unto an exceeding high mountain, and showeth him all the kingdoms of the world in a moment of time, and the glory of them.

And the devil said unto him, "To thee will I give all this authority, and the glory of them: for it hath been delivered unto me; and to whomsoever I will I give it. If thou therefore wilt worship before me, it shall all be thine."

Then saith Jesus unto him, "Get thee hence, Satan: for it is written. 'Thou shalt worship the Lord thy God, and him only shalt thou serve.'"

And when the devil had completed every temptation, he departed from him for a season; and behold, angels came and ministered unto him.

JOHN'S TESTIMONY TO JESUS.

And this is the witness of John, when the Jews sent unto him from Jerusalem priests and Levites to ask him, "Who art thou?" And he confessed and denied not; and he confessed, "I am not the Christ."

And they asked him, "What then? Art thou Elijah?"

And he saith, "I am not."

"Art thou the prophet?"

And he answered "No."

They said therefore unto him, "Who art thou? that we may give an answer to them that sent us? What sayest thou of thyself?"

He said, "I am the voice of one crying in the wilderness, 'Make straight the way of the Lord,' as said Isaiah the prophet."

And they had been sent from the Pharisees. And they asked him, and said unto him, "Why then baptizest thou, if thou art not the Christ, neither Elijah, neither the prophet."

John answered them, saying, "I baptize in water: in the midst of you standeth one whom ye know not, even he that cometh after me, the latchet of whose shoe I am not worthy to unloose."

These things were done in Bethany beyond the Jordan, where John was baptizing.

On the morrow he seeth Jesus coming unto him, and saith, "Behold, the Lamb of God, that taketh away the sin of the world! This is he of whom I said, 'After me cometh a man who is become before me: for he was before me.' And I knew him not; but that he should be made manifest to Israel, for this cause came I baptizing in water."

And John bare witness, saying, "I have beheld the Spirit descending as a dove out of heaven; and it abode upon him. And I knew him not: but he that sent me to baptize in water, he said unto me, 'Upon whomsoever thou shalt see the Spirit descending, and abiding upon him, the same is he that baptizeth in the Holy Spirit.' And I have seen, and have borne witness that this is the Son of God."

THE BEGINNINGS OF FAITH
THE FIRST DISCIPLES BY THE JORDAN.

Again on the morrow John was standing, and two of his disciples; and he looked upon Jesus as he walked and saith, "Behold, the Lamb of God!" And the two disciples heard him speak, and they followed Jesus.

And Jesus turned, and beheld them following, and saith unto them, "What seek ye?"

And they said unto him, "Rabbi" (which is to say, being interpreted, Teacher), "where abidest thou?"

He saith unto them, "Come, and ye shall see."

They came therefore and saw where he abode; and they abode with him that day: it was about the tenth hour.

One of the two that heard John speak, and followed him, was Andrew, Simon Peter's brother. He findeth first his own brother Simon, and saith unto him, "We have found the Messiah" (which is, being interpreted, Christ). He brought him unto

Jesus.

Jesus looked upon him, and said, "Thou art Simon the son of John: thou shalt be called Cephas" (which is by interpretation, Peter).

On the morrow he was minded to go forth into Galilee, and he findeth Philip: and Jesus saith unto him, "Follow me." Now Philip was from Bethsaida, of the city of Andrew and Peter. Philip findeth Nathanael, and saith unto him, "We have found him, of whom Moses in the law and the prophets, wrote, Jesus of Nazareth, the son of Joseph."

And Nathanael said unto him. "Can any good thing come out of Nazareth?"

Philip saith unto him, "Come and see."

Jesus saw Nathanael coming to him, and saith of him, "Behold, an Israelite indeed, in whom is no guile!"

Nathanael saith unto him, "Whence knowest thou me?"

Jesus answered and said unto him, "Before Philip called thee, when thou wast under the fig tree, I saw thee."

Nathanael answered him, "Rabbi, thou art the Son of God; thou art King of Israel."

Jesus answered and said unto him, "Because I said unto thee, 'I saw thee underneath the fig tree,' believest thou? thou shalt see greater things than these."

And he saith unto him, "Verily, verily, I say unto you, Ye shall see the heaven opened, and the angels of God ascending and descending upon the Son of man."

THE FIRST MIRACLE.

And the third day there was a marriage in Cana of Galilee; and the mother of Jesus was there: and Jesus also was bidden, and his disciples, to the marriage.

And when the wine failed, the mother of Jesus saith unto him, "They have no wine."

And Jesus saith unto her, "Woman, what have I to do with thee? mine hour is not yet come."

His mother saith unto the servants, "Whatsoever he saith unto you, do it."

Now there were six waterpots of stone set there after the Jews' manner of purifying, containing two or three firkins apiece. Jesus saith unto them, "Fill the waterpots with water."

And they filled them up to the brim.

And he saith unto them, "Draw out now, and bear unto the ruler of the feast."

And they bare it. And when the ruler of the feast tasted the water now become wine, and knew not whence it was (but the servants that had drawn the water knew), the ruler of the feast calleth the bridegroom, and saith unto him, "Every man setteth on first the good wine; and when men have drunk freely, then that which is worse: thou hast kept the good wine until now."

This beginning of his signs did Jesus in Cana of Galilee, and manifested his glory; and his disciples believed on him.

After this he went down to Capernaum, he, and his mother, and his brethren, and his disciples; and there they abode not many days.

JESUS IN JERUSALEM CLEANSING HIS FATHER'S HOUSE.

And the passover of the Jews was at hand, and Jesus went up to Jerusalem. And he found in the temple those that sold oxen and sheep and doves, and the changers of money sitting: and he made a scourge of cords, and cast all out of the temple, both the sheep and the oxen; and he poured out the changers' money, and overthrew their tables; and to them that sold the doves he said, "Take these things hence; make not my Father's house a house of merchandise."

His disciples remembered that it was written, "Zeal for thy house shall eat me up."

The Jews therefore answered and said unto him, "What sign showest thou unto us, seeing that thou doest these things?"

Jesus answered and said unto them, "Destroy this temple, and in three days I will raise it up."

The Jews therefore said, "Forty and six years was this temple in building, and wilt thou raise it up in three days?"

But he spake of the temple of his body. When therefore he was raised from the dead, his disciples remembered that he spake thus; and they believed the scripture, and the word which Jesus had said.

THE VISIT OF NICODEMUS.

Now when he was in Jerusalem at the passover, during the feast, many believed on his name, beholding his signs which he did. But Jesus did not trust himself unto them, for that he knew all men, and because he needed not that any one should bear witness concerning man; for he himself knew what was in man.

Now there was a man of the Pharisees, named Nicodemus, ruler of the Jews; the same came unto him by night, and said to him, "Rabbi, we know that thou art a teacher come from God; for no one can do these signs that thou doest, except God be with him."

Jesus answered and said unto him, "Verily, verily, I say unto thee, Except one be born anew, he cannot see the kingdom of God."

Nicodemus saith unto him, "How can a man be born when he is old? can he enter a second time into his mother's womb, and be born?"

Jesus answered, "Verily, verily, I say unto thee, Except one be born of water and the Spirit, he cannot enter into the kingdom of God. That which is born of the flesh is flesh: and that which is born of the Spirit is spirit. Marvel not that I said unto thee, 'Ye must be born anew.' The wind bloweth where it will, and thou hearest the voice thereof, but knowest not whence it cometh, and whither it goeth; so is every one that is born of the Spirit."

Nicodemus answered and said unto him, "How can these things be?"

Jesus answered and said unto him, "Art thou the teacher of Israel, and understandest not these things? Verily, verily, I say unto thee, We speak that which we know, and bear witness of that which we have seen; and ye receive not our witness. If I told you earthly things and ye believe not, how shall ye believe if I tell you heavenly things? And no one hath ascended into heaven but he that descended out of heaven, even the Son of man, who is in heaven. And as Moses lifted up the serpent in the wilderness even so must the Son of man be lifted up; that whosoever believeth may in him have eternal life.

"For God so loved the world, that he gave his only begotten Son, that whosoever believeth on him should not perish, but have eternal life. For God sent not the Son into the world to judge the world; but that the world should be saved through him. He that believeth on him is not judged: he that believeth not hath been judged already, because he hath not believed on the name of the only begotten Son of God. And this is the judgment, that the light is come into the world, and men loved the darkness rather than the light; for their works were evil. For every one that doeth evil hateth the light, and cometh not to the light, lest his works should be reproved. But he that doeth the truth cometh to the light, that his works may be made manifest, that they have been wrought in God."

PREPARATORY PREACHING
JESUS BAPTIZING AND PREACHING.

After these things came Jesus and his disciples into the land of Judaea; and there he tarried with them, and baptized (although Jesus himself baptized not, but his disciples).

And John also was baptizing in AEnon near to Salim, because there was much water there: and they came, and were baptized. For John was not yet cast into prison.

And Jesus himself, when he began to teach, was about thirty years of age.

JOHN'S TRIBUTE TO JESUS.

There arose therefore a questioning on the part of John's disciples with a Jew about purifying. And they came unto John, and said to him, "Rabbi, he that was with thee beyond the Jordan, to whom thou hast borne witness, behold, the same baptizeth, and all men come to him."

John answered and said, "A man can receive nothing, except it have been given him from heaven. Ye yourselves bear me witness, that I said, I am not the Christ, but, that I am sent before him. He that hath the bride is the bridegroom: but the friend of the bridegroom, that standeth and heareth him, rejoiceth greatly because of the bridegroom's voice: this my joy therefore is made full. He must increase, but I must decrease."

He that cometh from above is above all: he that is of the earth is of the earth, and of the earth he speaketh: he that cometh from heaven is above all. What he hath seen and heard, of that he beareth witness; and no man receiveth his witness. He that hath received his witness hath set his seal to this, that God is true. For he whom God hath sent speaketh the words of God: for he giveth not the Spirit by measure. The Father loveth the Son, and hath given all things into his hand. He that believeth on the Son hath eternal life; but he that obeyeth not the Son shall not see life, but the wrath of God abideth on him.

AT JACOB'S WELL.

When therefore the Lord knew that the Pharisees had heard that Jesus was making and baptizing more disciples than John, he left Judaea, and departed again into Galilee.

And he must needs pass through Samaria. So he cometh to a city of Samaria, called Sychar, near to the parcel of ground that Jacob gave to his son Joseph: and Jacob's well was there. Jesus therefore, being wearied with his journey, sat thus by the well. It was about the sixth hour.

There cometh a woman of Samaria to draw water: Jesus saith unto her, "Give me to drink." For his disciples were gone away into the city to buy food.

The Samaritan woman therefore saith unto him, "How is it that thou, being a Jew, askest drink of me, who am a Samaritan woman?" (for Jews have no dealings with Samaritans).

Jesus answered and said unto her, "If thou knewest the gift of God, and who it is that saith to thee, 'Give me to drink' thou wouldest have asked of him, and he would have given thee living water."

The woman saith unto him, "Sir, thou hast nothing to draw with, and the well is deep; whence then hast thou that living water? Art thou greater than our father Jacob, who gave us the well, and drank thereof himself, and his sons, and his cattle?"

Jesus answered and said unto her, "Every one that drinketh of this water shall thirst again; but whosoever drinketh of the water that I shall give him shall never thirst; but the water that I shall give him shall become in him a well of water, springing up unto eternal life."

The woman saith unto him, "Sir, give me this water, that I thirst not, neither come all the way hither to draw."

Jesus saith unto her, "Go, call thy husband, and come hither."

The woman answered and said unto him, "I have no husband."

Jesus saith unto her, "Thou saidst well, I have no husband: for thou hast had five husbands; and he whom thou now hast is not thy husband: this hast thou said truly."

The woman saith unto him, "Sir, I perceive that thou art a prophet. Our fathers worshipped in this mountain; and ye say, that in Jerusalem is the place where men ought to worship."

Jesus saith unto her, "Woman, believe me, the hour cometh, when neither in this mountain, nor in Jerusalem, shall ye worship the Father. Ye worship that which ye know not: we worship that which we know; for salvation is from the Jews. But the hour cometh, and now is, when the true worshippers shall worship the Father in spirit and truth: for such doth the Father seek to be his worshippers. God is a Spirit: and they that worship him must worship in spirit and truth."

The woman saith unto him, "I know that Messiah cometh (he that is called Christ): when he is come, he will declare unto us all things."

Jesus saith unto her, "I that speak unto thee am he."

PREACHING TO THE SAMARITANS.

And upon this came his disciples; and they marvelled that he was speaking with a woman; yet no man said, "What seekest thou?" or, "Why speakest thou with her?"

So the woman left her waterpot, and went away into the city, and saith to the people, "Come, see a man, who told me all things that ever I did: can this be the

Christ?"

They went out of the city, and were coming to him.

In the mean while the disciples prayed him, saying, "Rabbi, eat."

But he said unto them, "I have meat to eat that ye know not."

The disciples therefore said one to another, "Hath any man brought him aught to eat?"

Jesus saith unto them, "My meat is to do the will of him that sent me, and to accomplish his work. Say not ye, 'There are yet four months, and then cometh the harvest'? behold, I say unto you, Lift up your eyes and look on the fields, that they are white already unto harvest. He that reapeth receiveth wages, and gathereth fruit unto life eternal; that he that soweth and he that reapeth may rejoice together. For herein is the saying true, One soweth, and another reapeth. I sent you to reap that whereon ye have not labored: others have labored and ye are entered into their labor."

And from that city many of the Samaritans believed on him because of the word of the woman, who testified, "He told me all things that ever I did."

So when the Samaritans came unto him, they besought him to abide with them: and he abode there two days. And many more believed because of his word; and they said to the woman, "Now we believe, not because of thy speaking: for we have heard for ourselves, and know that this is indeed the Saviour of the world."

=HIS YEAR OF POPULARITY=

JESUS IN GALILEE
JOHN THE BAPTIST IMPRISONED.

Herod the tetrarch sent forth and laid hold upon John, and bound him in prison for the sake of Herodias, his brother Philip's wife; for he had married her. For John said unto Herod, "It is not lawful for thee to have thy brother's wife."

And Herodias set herself against him, and desired to kill him: and she could not; for Herod feared John, knowing that he was a righteous and holy man, and kept him safe.

And when he would have put him to death, he feared the multitude, because they counted him as a prophet.

RECEPTION OF JESUS BY THE GALILAEANS.

Now when Jesus heard that John was delivered up, he returned in the power of the Spirit into Galilee, and the Galilaeans received him, having seen all the things that he did in Jerusalem at the feast: for they also went unto the feast.

And a fame went out concerning him through all the region round about. And he taught in their synagogues, preaching the gospel of God, and saying, "The time is fulfilled, and the kingdom of God is at hand: repent ye, and believe in the gospel."

HEALING THE NOBLEMAN'S SON.

He came therefore again unto Cana of Galilee, where he made the water wine. And there was a certain nobleman, whose son was sick at Capernaum. When he heard that Jesus was come out of Judaea into Galilee, he went unto him, and besought him that he would come down, and heal his son; for he was at the point of death.

Jesus therefore said unto him, "Except ye see signs and wonders, ye will in no wise believe."

The nobleman saith unto him, "Sir, come down ere my child die."

Jesus saith unto him, "Go thy way; thy son liveth."

The man believed the word that Jesus spake unto him, and he went his way. And as he was now going down, his servants met him, saying that his son lived. So he inquired of them the hour when he began to amend.

They said therefore unto him, "Yesterday at the seventh hour the fever left him."

So the father knew that it was at that hour in which Jesus said unto him, "Thy son liveth": and himself believed, and his whole house.

This is again the second sign that Jesus did, having come out of Judaea into Galilee.

THE RECALL OF THE FISHERMEN.

And he came down to Capernaum, a city of Galilee, which is by the sea, in the borders of Zebulun and Naphtali: that it might be fulfilled which was spoken through Isaiah the prophet, saying,

"The land of Zebulun and the land of Naphtali,
Toward the sea, beyond the Jordan,
Galilee of the Gentiles,

The people that sat in darkness
Saw a great light,
And to them that sat in the region and shadow of death,
To them did light spring up."

Now it came to pass, while the multitude pressed upon him and heard the word of God, that he was standing by the lake of Gennesaret; and he saw two boats standing by the lake: but the fishermen had gone out of them, and were washing their nets. And he entered into one of the boats, which was Simon's, and asked him to put out a little from the land. And he sat down and taught the multitudes out of the boat.

And when he had left speaking, he said unto Simon, "Put out into the deep, and let down your nets for a draught."

And Simon answered and said, "Master, we toiled all night, and took nothing: but at thy word I will let down the nets."

And when they had done this, they inclosed a great multitude of fishes; and their nets were breaking; and they beckoned unto their partners in the other boat, that they should come and help them. And they came, and filled both the boats, so that they began to sink.

But Simon Peter, when he saw it, fell down at Jesus' knees, saying, "Depart from me; for I am a sinful man, O Lord!"

For he was amazed, and all that were with him, at the draught of the fishes which they had taken; and so were also James and John, sons of Zebedee, who were partners with Simon. And Jesus said unto Simon, "Fear not; from henceforth thou shalt catch men."

And when they had brought their boats to land, they left all, and followed him.

A DAY OF GOOD DEEDS IN CAPERNAUM.

And straightway on the sabbath day he entered into the synagogue and taught. And they were astonished at his teaching. for his word was with authority.

And in the synagogue there was a man, that had a spirit of an unclean demon; and he cried out with a loud voice, "Ah! what have we to do with thee, Jesus thou Nazarene? art thou come to destroy us? I know thee who thou art, the Holy One of God!"

And Jesus rebuked him, saying, "Hold thy peace, and come out of him."

And when the demon had thrown him down in the midst, tearing him and crying out with a loud voice, he came out of him, having done him no hurt.

And amazement came upon all, and they spake together, one with another, saying, "What is this word? for with authority and power he commandeth the unclean spirits, and they come out."

And there went forth a rumor concerning him into every place of the region of Galilee round about.

And he rose up from the synagogue. and entered into the house of Simon. And Simon's wife's mother was holden with a great fever; and they besought him for her. And he stood over her, and rebuked the fever; and it left her: and immediately she rose up and ministered unto them.

And at even, when the sun did set, they brought unto him all that were sick, and them that were possessed with demons. And all the city was gathered together at the door. And he cast out many demons with a word, and he suffered not the demons to speak, because they knew that he was the Christ. And he laid his hands on every one of them, and healed all that were sick of divers diseases; that it might be fulfilled which was spoken through Isaiah the prophet, saying, "Himself took our infirmities, and bare our diseases."

THE FIRST LEPER HEALED.

And in the morning, a great while before day, he rose up and went out, and departed into a desert place, and there prayed. And Simon and they that were with him followed after him; and they found him, and say unto him, "All are seeking thee."

And he saith unto them, "Let us go elsewhere into the next towns, that I may preach there also; for to this end came I forth."

And he went into their synagogues throughout all Galilee, preaching and casting out demons.

And it came to pass, while he was in one of the cities, there cometh to him a man full of leprosy, beseeching him, and kneeling down to him, and saying unto him, "Lord, if thou wilt, thou canst make me clean."

And being moved with compassion, he stretched forth his hand, and touched him, and saith unto him, "I will; be thou made clean." And straightway the leprosy departed from him, and he was made clean. And he strictly charged him, and straightway sent him out, and saith unto him, "See thou say nothing to any man: but go show thyself to the priest, and offer for thy cleansing the things which Moses commanded, for a testimony unto them."

But he went out, and began to publish it much, and to spread abroad the matter, insomuch that Jesus could no more openly enter into a city, but withdrew himself to desert places and prayed: and they came to him from every quarter to hear and to be healed of their infirmities. And the power of the Lord was with him to heal.

BEGINNINGS OF CONTROVERSY
THE HEALING OF A PARALYTIC.

And when he entered again into Capernaum after some days, it was noised that he was in the house. And many were gathered together, so that there was no longer room for them, no, not even about the door; and he spake the word unto them.

And they come, bringing unto him a man sick of the palsy, borne of four. And when they could not come nigh unto him for the crowd, they went up to the house-top, and uncovered the roof where he was: and when they had broken it up, they let down the bed whereon the sick of the palsy lay.

And Jesus seeing their faith saith unto the sick of the palsy, "Son, thy sins are forgiven."

But there were certain of the scribes sitting there, and reasoning in their hearts, "Why doth this man thus speak? he blasphemeth: who can forgive sins but one, even God?"

And straightway Jesus, perceiving in his spirit that they so reasoned within themselves, saith unto them, "Why reason ye these things in your hearts? Which is easier, to say to the sick of the palsy, 'Thy sins are forgiven,' or to say, 'Arise, and take up thy bed, and walk?' But that ye may know that the Son of man hath author-ity on earth to forgive sins (he saith to the sick of the palsy), 'I say unto thee, Arise, take up thy bed, and go unto thy house.'"

And he arose, and straightway took up the bed, and went forth before them all; insomuch that they were all amazed, and were filled with fear, and glorified God, saying, "We never saw it on this fashion: we have seen strange things to-day."

THE PUBLICAN DISCIPLE.

And Jesus went forth again by the sea side; and all the multitude resorted unto him, and he taught them. And as he passed by, he saw a man, called Levi Matthew, the son of Alphaeus, sitting at the place of toll, and he saith unto him, "Follow me."

And he forsook all, and arose and followed him.

And Levi made him a great feast in his house. And there was a great multitude of publicans and sinners that were sitting at meat with Jesus and his disciples.

And when the Pharisees saw it, they said unto his disciples, "Why eateth your Teacher with the publicans and sinners?"

But when he heard it, he said, "They that are whole have no need of a physi-cian, but they that are sick. But go ye and learn what this meaneth, 'I desire mercy, and not sacrifice': for I came not to call the righteous, but sinners."

THE OLD AND THE NEW.

And John's disciples and the Pharisees were fasting, and they come and say unto him, "The disciples of John fast often, and make supplications; likewise also the disciples of the Pharisees; but thine eat and drink."

And Jesus said unto them, "Can ye make the sons of the bride-chamber fast, while the bridegroom is with them? But the days will come; and when the bridegroom shall be taken away from them, then will they fast in those days."

And he spake also a parable unto them: "No man rendeth a piece from a new garment and putteth it upon an old garment; else he will rend the new, and also the piece from the new will not agree with the old. And no man putteth new wine into old wine-skins; else the new wine will burst the skins, and itself will be spilled, and the skins will perish. But new wine must be put into fresh wine-skins. And no man having drunk old wine desireth new; for he saith, The old is good."

A SABBATH HEALING IN JERUSALEM.

After these things there was a feast of the Jews; and Jesus went up to Jerusalem.

Now there is in Jerusalem by the sheep gate a pool, which is called in Hebrew Bethesda, having five porches. In these lay a multitude of them that were sick, blind, halt, withered. And a certain man was there, who had been thirty and eight years in his infirmity. When Jesus saw him lying, and knew that he had been now a long time in that case, he saith unto him, "Wouldest thou be made whole?"

The sick man answered him, "Sir, I have no man, when the water is troubled, to put me into the pool: but while I am coming, another steppeth down before me."

Jesus saith unto him, "Arise, take up thy bed, and walk."

And straightway the man was made whole, and took up his bed and walked. Now it was the sabbath on that day.

So the Jews said unto him that was cured, "It is the sabbath, and it is not lawful for thee to take up thy bed."

But he answered them, "He that made me whole, the same said unto me, 'Take up thy bed, and walk.'"

They asked him, "Who is the man that said unto thee, 'Take up thy bed, and walk'?"

But he that was healed knew not who it was; for Jesus had conveyed himself away, a multitude being in the place. Afterward Jesus findeth him in the temple, and said unto him, "Behold, thou art made whole: sin no more, lest a worse thing befall thee."

The man went away, and told the Jews that it was Jesus who had made him whole. And for this cause the Jews persecuted Jesus, because he did these things on the sabbath.

But Jesus answered them, "My Father worketh even until now, and I work."

For this cause therefore the Jews sought the more to kill him, because he not only brake the sabbath, but also called God his own Father, making himself equal with God.

Jesus therefore answered and said unto them, "Verily, verily, I say unto you, The Son can do nothing of himself, but what he seeth the Father doing: for what things soever he doeth, these the Son also doeth in like manner. For the Father loveth the Son, and showeth him all things that himself doeth: and greater works than these will he show him, that ye may marvel. For as the Father raiseth the dead and giveth them life, even so the Son also giveth life to whom he will. For neither doth the Father judge any man, but he hath given all judgment unto the Son; that all may honor the Son, even as they honor the Father. He that honoreth not the Son honoreth not the Father that sent him. Verily, verily, I say unto you, He that heareth my word, and believeth him that sent me, hath eternal life, and cometh not into judgment, but hath passed out of death into life. Verily, verily, I say unto you, The hour cometh, and now is, when the dead shall hear the voice of the Son of God; and they that hear shall live. For as the Father hath life in himself, even so gave he to the Son also to have life in himself: and he gave him authority to execute judgment, because he is a son of man. Marvel not at this: for the hour cometh, in which all that are in the tombs shall hear his voice, and shall come forth; they that have done good, unto the resurrection of life; and they that have done evil, unto the resurrection of judgment.

"I can of myself do nothing: as I hear, I judge: and my judgment is righteous; because I seek not mine own will, but the will of him that sent me. If I bear witness of myself, my witness is not true. It is another that beareth witness of me; and I know that the witness which he witnesseth of me is true. Ye have sent unto John, and he hath borne witness unto the truth. But the witness which I receive is not from man: howbeit I say these things, that ye may be saved. He was the lamp that burneth and shineth; and ye were willing to rejoice for a season in his light. But the witness which I have is greater than that of John; for the works which the Father hath given me to accomplish, the very works that I do, bear witness of me, that the Father hath sent me. And the Father that sent me, he hath borne witness of me. Ye have neither heard his voice at any time, nor seen his form. And ye have not his word abiding in you: for whom he sent, him ye believe not.

"Ye search the scriptures, because ye think that in them ye have eternal life; and these are they which bear witness of me; and ye will not come to me, that ye may have life. I receive not glory from men. But I know you, that ye have not the love of God in yourselves. I am come in my Father's name, and ye receive me not: if another shall come in his own name, him ye will receive. How can ye believe, who receive glory one of another, and the glory that cometh from the only God ye seek not? Think not that I will accuse you to the Father: there is one that accuseth you, even Moses, on whom ye have set your hope. For if ye believed Moses, ye would believe me; for he wrote of me. But if ye believe not his writings, how shall ye believe my words?"

PLUCKING GRAIN ON THE SABBATH.

At that season Jesus went on the sabbath day through the grainfields; and his disciples were hungry and began to pluck ears and to eat, rubbing them in their hands.

But the Pharisees, when they saw it, said unto him, "Behold, thy disciples do that which it is not lawful to do upon the sabbath."

But he said unto them, "Have ye not read what David did, when he had need and was hungry, and they that were with him: how he entered into the house of God, and ate the showbread, which it was not lawful for him to eat, neither for them that were with him, but only for the priests? Or have ye not read in the law, that on the sabbath day the priests in the temple profane the sabbath, and are guiltless? But I say unto you, that one greater than the temple is here. But if ye had known what this meaneth, 'I desire mercy, and not sacrifice,' ye would not have condemned the guiltless."

And he said unto them, "The sabbath was made for man, and not man for the sabbath: so that the Son of man is lord even of the sabbath."

MANY CALLED AND FEW CHOSEN
A MULTITUDE OF DISCIPLES.

And the report of him went forth into all Syria: and they brought unto him all that were sick, holden with divers diseases and torments, possessed with demons, and epileptic, and palsied; and he healed them.

And Jesus with his disciples withdrew to the sea: and a great multitude from Galilee followed; and from Judaea, and from Jerusalem, and from Idumaea, and beyond the Jordan, and about Tyre and Sidon, a great multitude, hearing what great things he did, came unto him.

And he spake to his disciples, that a little boat should wait on him because of the crowd, lest they should throng him: for he had healed many; insomuch that as many as had plagues pressed upon him that they might touch him: for power came forth from him, and healed them all.

And the unclean spirits, whensoever they beheld him, fell down before him, and cried, saying, "Thou art the Son of God."

And he charged them much that they should not make him known: that it might be fulfilled which was spoken through Isaiah the prophet, saying,

"Behold my servant whom I have chosen;
My beloved in whom my soul is well pleased;

I will put my Spirit upon him,
And he shall declare judgment to the Gentiles.
He shall not strive, nor cry aloud;
Neither shall any one hear his voice in the streets.
A bruised reed shall he not break.
And smoking flax shall he not quench.
Till he send forth judgment unto victory.
And in his name shall the nations hope."

SELECTION OF THE TWELVE.

And it came to pass in these days, that he went out into the mountain to pray; and he continued all night in prayer to God. And when it was day, he called his disciples; and he chose from them twelve, that they might be with him, and that he might send them forth to preach, and to have authority to cast out demons.

Now the names of the twelve apostles are these: Simon, whom he surnamed Peter, and Andrew, his brother; James, the son of Zebedee, and John his brother, and them he surnamed Boanerges, which is sons of thunder; Philip and Bartholomew; Thomas and Matthew the publican; James the son of Alphaeus, and Thaddaeus; Simon, who was called the Zealot, and Judas Iscariot, who became a traitor.

THE TEACHING OF THE KINGDOM
THE CITIZENS OF THE KINGDOM.

And he lifted up his eyes on his disciples, and said:
"Blessed are the poor in spirit: for theirs is the kingdom of heaven.
"Blessed are they that mourn: for they shall be comforted.
"Blessed are the meek: for they shall inherit the earth.
"Blessed are they that hunger and thirst after righteousness: for they shall be filled.
"Blessed are the merciful: for they shall obtain mercy.

"Blessed are the pure in heart: for they shall see God.

"Blessed are the peacemakers: for they shall be called sons of God.

"Blessed are they that have been persecuted for righteousness' sake: for theirs is the kingdom of heaven. Blessed are ye when men shall reproach you, and persecute you, and say all manner of evil against you falsely, for my sake. Rejoice, and be exceeding glad: for great is your reward in heaven: for so persecuted they the prophets that were before you.

"Ye are the salt of the earth: but if the salt have lost its savor, wherewith shall it be salted? it is thenceforth good for nothing, but to be cast out and trodden under foot of men.

"Ye are the light of the world. A city set on a hill cannot be hid. Neither do men light a lamp, and put it under the bushel, but on the stand; and it shineth unto all that are in the house. Even so let your light shine before men; that they may see your good works, and glorify your Father who is in heaven.

THE RIGHTEOUSNESS OF THE KINGDOM.

"Think not that I came to destroy the law or the prophets: I came not to destroy, but to fulfil. For verily I say unto you, Till heaven and earth pass away, one jot or one tittle shall in no wise pass away from the law, till all things be accomplished. Whosoever therefore shall break one of these least commandments, and shall teach men so, shall be called least in the kingdom of heaven: but whosoever shall do and teach them, he shall be called great in the kingdom of heaven. For I say unto you, that except your righteousness shall exceed the righteousness of the scribes and Pharisees, ye shall in no wise enter into the kingdom of heaven.

"Ye have heard that it was said to them of old time, 'Thou shalt not kill; and whosoever shall kill shall be in danger of the judgment:' but I say unto you, that every one who is angry with his brother shall be in danger of the judgment; and whosoever shall say to his brother, 'Raca,' shall be in danger of the council; and whosoever shall say, 'Thou fool,' shall be in danger of the hell of fire.

"If therefore thou art offering thy gift at the altar, and there rememberest that thy brother hath aught against thee, leave there thy gift before the altar, and go thy way, first be reconciled to thy brother, and then come and offer thy gift. Agree with thine adversary quickly, while thou art with him in the way; lest haply the adversary deliver thee to the judge, and the judge deliver thee to the officer, and thou be cast into prison. Verily I say unto thee, Thou shalt by no means come out thence, till thou have paid the last farthing.

"Ye have heard that it was said, 'Thou shalt not commit adultery:' but I say unto you, that every one that looketh on a woman to lust after her hath committed adultery with her already in his heart. And if thy right eye causeth thee to stumble, pluck it out, and cast it from thee: for it is profitable for thee that one of thy members should perish, and not thy whole body be cast into hell. And if thy right hand causeth thee to stumble, cut it off, and cast it from thee: for it is profitable for thee that one of thy members should perish, and not thy whole body go into hell.

"It was said also, 'Whosoever shall put away his wife, let him give her a writing of divorcement:' but I say unto you, that every one that putteth away his wife, saving for the cause of fornication, maketh her an adulteress: and whosoever shall marry her when she is put away committeth adultery.

"Again, ye have heard that it was said to them of old time, 'Thou shalt not forswear thyself, but shalt perform unto the Lord thine oaths:' but I say unto you, Swear not at all; neither by the heaven, for it is the throne of God; nor by the earth, for it is the footstool of his feet; nor by Jerusalem, for it is the city of the great King. Neither shalt thou swear by thy head, for thou canst not make one hair white or black. But let your speech be, 'Yea, yea; Nay, nay:' and whatsoever is more than these is of the evil one.

"Ye have heard that it was said, 'An eye for an eye, and a tooth for a tooth:' but I say unto you, Resist not him that is evil: but whosoever smiteth thee on thy right cheek, turn to him the other also. And if any man would go to law with thee, and take away thy coat, let him have thy cloak also. And whosoever shall compel thee to go one mile, go with him two. Give to every one that asketh thee; and of him that taketh away thy goods ask them not again, and from him that would borrow of thee turn not thou away. All things therefore whatsoever ye would that men should do unto you, even so do ye also unto them: for this is the law and the prophets.

"Ye have heard that it was said, 'Thou shalt love thy neighbor, and hate thine enemy:' but I say unto you, Love your enemies, do good to them that hate you, bless them that curse you, pray for them that despitefully use you, that ye may be sons of your Father who is in heaven: for he maketh his sun to rise on the evil and the good, and sendeth rain on the just and the unjust. For if ye love them that love you, what reward have ye? do not even the publicans the same? And if ye salute your brethren only, what do ye more than others? do not even the Gentiles the same? And if ye do good to them that do good to you, what thank have ye? for even sinners do the same. And if ye lend to them of whom ye hope to receive, what thank have ye? even sinners lend to sinners, to receive again as much. But love your enemies, and do them good, and lend, never despairing; and your reward shall be great, and ye shall be sons of the Most High: for he is kind toward the unthankful and evil. Ye therefore shall be perfect, as your heavenly Father is perfect.

THE DANGER OF HYPOCRISY.

"Take heed that ye do not your righteousness before men, to be seen of them: else ye have no reward with your Father who is in heaven.

"When therefore thou doest alms, sound not a trumpet before thee, as the hypocrites do in the synagogues and in the streets, that they may have glory of men. Verily I say unto you, They have received their reward. But when thou doest alms, let not thy left hand know what thy right hand doeth: that thine alms may be in secret: and thy Father who seeth in secret shall recompense thee.

"And when ye pray, ye shall not be as the hypocrites: for they love to stand and pray in the synagogues and in the corners of the streets, that they may be seen of men. Verily I say unto you, They have received their reward. But thou, when thou prayest, enter into thine inner chamber, and having shut thy door, pray to thy Father who is in secret, and thy Father who seeth in secret shall recompense thee. And in praying use not vain repetitions, as the Gentiles do: for they think that they shall be heard for their much speaking. Be not therefore like unto them: for your Father knoweth what things ye have need of before ye ask him. After this manner therefore pray ye:

Our Father who art in heaven,
Hallowed be thy name.
Thy kingdom come.
Thy will be done, as in heaven, so on earth.
Give us this day our daily bread.
And forgive us our debts, as we also have forgiven our debtors.
And bring us not into temptation, but deliver us from evil.

"For if ye forgive men their trespasses, your heavenly Father will also forgive you. But if ye forgive not men their trespasses, neither will your Father forgive your trespasses.

"Moreover when ye fast, be not, as the hypocrites, of a sad countenance: for they disfigure their faces, that they may be seen of men to fast. Verily I say unto you, They have received their reward. But thou, when thou fastest, anoint thy head, and wash thy face; that thou be not seen of men to fast, but of thy Father who is in secret: and thy Father, who seeth in secret, shall recompense thee.

SIMPLE TRUST IN GOD.

"Lay not up for yourselves treasures upon the earth, where moth and rust consume, and where thieves break through and steal: but lay up for yourselves treasures in heaven, where neither moth nor rust doth consume, and where thieves do not break through nor steal: for where thy treasure is, there will thy heart be also.

"The lamp of the body is the eye: if therefore thine eye be single, thy whole body shall be full of light. But if thine eye be evil, thy whole body shall be full of darkness. If therefore the light that is in thee be darkness, how great is the darkness!

"No man can serve two masters: for either he will hate the one, and love the other; or else he will hold to one, and despise the other. Ye cannot serve God and mammon.

"Therefore I say unto you, Be not anxious for your life, what ye shall eat, or what ye shall drink; nor yet for your body, what ye shall put on. Is not the life more than the food, and the body than the raiment? Behold the birds of the heaven, that they sow not, neither do they reap, nor gather into barns; and your heavenly Father feedeth them. Are not ye of much more value than they? And which of you by being anxious can add one cubit unto the measure of his life?

"And why are ye anxious concerning raiment? Consider the lilies of the field, how they grow; they toil not, neither do they spin: yet I say unto you, that even Solomon in all his glory was not arrayed like one of these. But if God doth so clothe the grass of the field, which to-day is, and to-morrow is cast into the oven, shall he not much more clothe you, O ye of little faith? Be not therefore anxious, saying, 'What shall we eat?' or, 'What shall we drink?' or, 'Wherewithal shall we be clothed?' For after all these things do the Gentiles seek; for your heavenly Father knoweth that ye have need of all these things. But seek ye first his kingdom, and his righteousness; and all these things shall be added unto you. Fear not, little flock; for it is your Father's good pleasure to give you the kingdom.

"Be not therefore anxious for the morrow: for the morrow will be anxious for itself. Sufficient unto the day is the evil thereof.

CHARITABLE JUDGMENT.

"Be ye merciful, even as your Father is merciful. And judge not, and ye shall not be judged: and condemn not, and ye shall not be condemned: release, and ye shall be released: give, and it shall be given unto you; good measure, pressed down, shaken together, running over, shall they give into your bosom. For with what measure ye mete it shall be measured to you again."

And he spake also a parable unto them, "Can the blind guide the blind? shall they not both fall into a pit? The disciple is not above his teacher: but every one when he is perfected shall be as his teacher. And why beholdest thou the mote that is in thy brother's eye, but considerest not the beam that is in thine own eye? Or how canst thou say to thy brother, 'Brother, let me cast out the mote that is in thine eye,' when thou thyself beholdest not the beam that is in thine own eye? Thou hypocrite, cast out first the beam out of thine own eye, and then shalt thou see clearly to cast out the mote that is in thy brother's eye.

"Give not that which is holy unto the dogs, neither cast your pearls before the swine, lest haply they trample them under their feet, and turn and rend you."

PRAYER.

And he said unto them, "Which of you shall have a friend, and shall go unto him at midnight, and say to him, 'Friend, lend me three loaves; for a friend of mine is come to me from a journey, and I have nothing to set before him;' and he from within shall answer and say, 'Trouble me not: the door is now shut, and my children are with me in bed; I cannot rise and give thee?' I say unto you, Though he will not rise and give him because he is his friend, yet because of his importunity he will arise and give him as many as he needeth.

"And I say unto you, Ask, and it shall be given you; seek, and ye shall find; knock, and it shall be opened unto you: for every one that asketh receiveth; and he that seeketh findeth; and to him that knocketh it shall be opened. Or what man is there of you that is a father, who, if his son shall ask him for a loaf, will give him a stone; or if he shall ask for a fish, will give him a serpent; or if he shall ask an egg, will give him a scorpion? If ye then, being evil, know how to give good gifts unto your children, how much more shall your Father who is in heaven give good things to them that ask him?

SINCERITY.

"Enter ye in by the narrow gate: for wide is the gate, and broad is the way, that leadeth to destruction, and many are they that enter in thereby. For narrow is the gate, and straitened the way, that leadeth unto life, and few are they that find it.

"Beware of false prophets, who come to you in sheep's clothing, but inwardly are ravening wolves. By their fruits ye shall know them. Do men gather grapes of thorns, or figs of thistles? Even so every good tree bringeth forth good fruit; but the corrupt tree bringeth forth evil fruit. A good tree cannot bring forth evil fruit, neither can a corrupt tree bring forth good fruit. Every tree that bringeth not forth good fruit is hewn down, and cast into the fire. Therefore by their fruits ye shall know them.

"The good man out of the good treasure of his heart bringeth forth that which is good; and the evil man out of the evil treasure bringeth forth that which is evil: for out of the abundance of the heart his mouth speaketh.

"Not every one that saith unto me, 'Lord, Lord,' shall enter into the kingdom of heaven; but he that doeth the will of my Father who is in heaven. Many will say to me in that day, 'Lord, Lord, did we not prophesy by thy name, and by thy name cast out demons, and by thy name do many mighty works?' And then will I profess unto them, I never knew you: depart from me, ye that work iniquity.

"Every one therefore that heareth these words of mine, and doeth them, shall be likened unto a wise man, who built his house upon the rock: and the rain descended, and the floods came, and the winds blew, and beat upon that house; and it fell not: for it was founded upon the rock. And every one that heareth these words of mine, and doeth them not, shall be likened unto a foolish man, who built his house upon the sand: and the rain descended, and the floods came, and the winds blew, and smote upon that house; and it fell: and great was the fall thereof."

And it came to pass, when Jesus had finished these words, the multitudes were astonished at his teaching: for he taught them as one having authority, and not as their scribes.

A TOUR IN GALILEE
THE WORTHY CENTURION.

After he had ended all his sayings in the ears of the people, he entered into Capernaum.

And a certain centurion's servant, who was dear unto him, was sick and at the point of death. And when he heard concerning Jesus, he sent unto him elders of the Jews, asking him that he would come and save his servant.

And they, when they came to Jesus, besought him earnestly, saying, "He is worthy that thou shouldest do this for him; for he loveth our nation, and himself built us our synagogue."

And Jesus went with them. And when he was now not far from the house, the centurion sent friends to him, saying unto him, "Lord, trouble not thyself; for I am not worthy that thou shouldest come under my roof: wherefore neither thought I myself worthy to come unto thee: but say the word, and my servant shall be healed. For I also am a man set under authority, having under myself soldiers: and I say to this one, 'Go,' and he goeth; and to another, 'Come,' and he cometh; and to my servant, 'Do this,' and he doeth it."

And when Jesus heard these things, he marvelled at him, and turned and said unto the multitude that followed him, "Verily I say unto you, I have not found so great faith, no, not in Israel. And I say unto you, that many shall come from the east and the west, and shall sit down with Abraham, and Isaac, and Jacob, in the kingdom of heaven: but the sons of the kingdom shall be cast forth into the outer darkness: there shall be the weeping and the gnashing of teeth."

And they that were sent, returning to the house, found the servant whole.

RAISING THE WIDOW'S SON.

And it came to pass soon afterwards, that he went to a city called Nain; and his disciples went with him, and a great multitude. Now when he drew near to the gate of the city, behold, there was carried out one that was dead, the only son of his mother, and she was a widow: and much people of the city was with her.

And when the Lord saw her, he had compassion on her, and said unto her, "Weep not."

And he came nigh and touched the bier: and the bearers stood still. And he said, "Young man, I say unto thee, Arise."

And he that was dead sat up, and began to speak. And he gave him to his mother.

And fear took hold on all: and they glorified God, saying, "A great prophet is arisen among us: and, God hath visited his people."

And this report went forth concerning him in the whole of Judaea, and all the region round about.

A QUESTION FROM JOHN THE BAPTIST.

And the disciples of John told him in the prison of all these things. And John calling unto him two of his disciples sent them to the Lord, saying, "Art thou he that cometh, or look we for another?"

And when the men were come unto him, they said, "John the Baptist hath sent us unto thee, saying, 'Art thou he that cometh, or look we for another?'"

In that hour he cured many of diseases and plagues and evil spirits; and on many that were blind he bestowed sight. And he answered and said unto them, "Go and tell John the things which ye have seen and heard; the blind receive their sight, the lame walk, the lepers are cleansed, and the deaf hear, the dead are raised up, the poor have good tidings preached to them. And blessed is he, whosoever shall find no occasion of stumbling in me."

JESUS' ESTIMATE OF JOHN THE BAPTIST.

And when the messengers of John were departed, he began to say unto the multitudes concerning John, "What went ye out into the wilderness to behold? a reed shaken with the wind? But what went ye out to see? a man clothed in soft raiment? Behold, they that are gorgeously apparelled, and live delicately, are in kings' courts. But what went ye out to see? a prophet? Yea, I say unto you, and much more than a prophet. This is he of whom it is written.

"'Behold, I send my messenger before thy face,
Who shall prepare thy way before thee.'

"Verily I say unto you, Among them that are born of women there hath not arisen a greater than John the Baptist: yet he that is but little in the kingdom of heaven is greater than he. And all the people when they heard, and the publicans, justified God, being baptized with the baptism of John. But the Pharisees and the lawyers rejected for themselves the counsel of God, being not baptized of him.

"And from the days of John the Baptist until now the kingdom of heaven suffereth violence, and men of violence take it by force. For all the prophets and the law prophesied until John. And if ye are willing to receive it, this is Elijah that is to come. He that hath ears to hear, let him hear.

"But whereunto shall I liken this generation? It is like unto children sitting in the marketplaces, who call unto their fellows and say, 'We piped unto you, and ye did not dance; we wailed, and ye did not mourn.' For John came neither eating nor drinking, and they say, 'He hath a demon.' The Son of man came eating and drinking, and they say, 'Behold, a gluttonous man and a winebibber, a friend of publicans and sinners!' And wisdom is justified of all her children."

THE DEATH OF JOHN THE BAPTIST.

And Herod on his birthday made a supper to his lords, and the high captains, and the chief men of Galilee. And the daughter of Herodias danced in the midst, and pleased Herod, and them that sat at meat with him; and the king said unto the damsel, "Ask of me whatsoever thou wilt, and I will give it thee."

And he sware unto her, "Whatsoever thou shalt ask of me, I will give it to thee, unto the half of my kingdom."

And she went out, and said unto her mother, "What shall I ask?"

And she said, "The head of John the Baptist."

And she came in straightway with haste unto the king, and asked, saying, "I will that thou forthwith give me on a platter the head of John the Baptist."

And the king was exceeding sorry; but for the sake of his oaths, and of them that sat at meat, he would not reject her. And straightway the king sent forth a soldier of his guard, and commanded to bring his head: and he went and beheaded him in the prison, and brought his head on a platter, and gave it to the damsel; and the damsel gave it to her mother.

And when his disciples heard thereof, they came and took up his corpse, and laid it in a tomb; and they went and told Jesus.

FORGIVENESS OF THE REPENTANT WOMAN.

And one of the Pharisees desired him that he would eat with him. And he entered into the Pharisee's house, and sat down to meat. And behold, a woman who was in the city, a sinner; and when she knew that he was sitting at meat in the Pharisee's house, she brought an alabaster cruse of ointment, and standing behind at his feet, weeping, she began to wet his feet with her tears, and wiped them with the hair of her head, and kissed his feet, and anointed them with the ointment.

Now when the Pharisee that had bidden him saw it, he spake within himself, saying, "This man, if he were a prophet, would have perceived who and what manner of woman this is that toucheth him, that she is a sinner."

And Jesus answering said unto him, "Simon, I have somewhat to say unto thee."

And he saith, "Teacher, say on."

"A certain lender had two debtors: the one owed five hundred shillings, and the other fifty. When they had not wherewith to pay, he forgave them both. Which of them therefore will love him most?"

Simon answered and said, "He, I suppose, to whom he forgave the most."

And he said unto him, "Thou hast rightly judged." And turning to the woman, he said unto Simon, "Seest thou this woman? I entered into thy house, thou gavest me no water for my feet: but she hath wetted my feet with her tears, and wiped them with her hair. Thou gavest me no kiss: but she, since the time I came in, hath not ceased to kiss my feet. My head with oil thou didst not anoint: but she hath anointed my feet with ointment. Wherefore I say unto thee, Her sins, which are many, are forgiven; for she loved much: but to whom little is forgiven, the same loveth little."

And he said unto her, "Thy sins are forgiven."

And they that sat at meat with him began to say within themselves, "Who is this that even forgiveth sins?"

And he said unto the woman, "Thy faith hath saved thee; go in peace."

THE MINISTERING WOMEN.

And it came to pass soon afterwards, that he went about through cities and villages, preaching and bringing the good tidings of the kingdom of God, and with him the twelve, and certain women who had been healed of evil spirits and infirmities: Mary that was called Magdalene, from whom seven demons had gone out, and Joanna the wife of Chuzas Herod's steward, and Susanna, and many others, who ministered unto them of their substance.

GROWING POPULARITY AND
RISING OPPOSITION
THE CONCERN OF JESUS' FRIENDS.

And he cometh into a house. And the multitude cometh together again, so that they could not so much as eat bread. And when his friends heard it, they went out to lay hold on him: for they said, "He is beside himself."

And there came to him his mother and brethren, and they could not come at him for the crowd. And it was told him, "Thy mother and thy brethren stand without, desiring to see thee."

But he answered and said unto him that told him, "Who is my mother? and who are my brethren?" And he stretched forth his hand towards his disciples, and said, "Behold, my mother and my brethren! For whosoever shall do the will of my Father who is in heaven, he is my brother, and sister, and mother."

WARNING OF ETERNAL SIN.

Then was brought unto him one possessed with a demon, blind and dumb: and he healed him, insomuch that the dumb man spake and saw. And all the multitudes were amazed, and said, "Can this be the son of David?"

But when the Pharisees heard it, and the scribes that came down from Jerusalem, they said, "This man doth not cast out demons, but by Beelzebub the prince of the demons."

And knowing their thoughts he said unto them, "Every kingdom divided against itself is brought to desolation; and every city or house divided against itself shall not stand: and if Satan casteth out Satan, he is divided against himself; how then shall his kingdom stand? And if I by Beelzebub cast out demons, by whom do your sons cast them out? therefore shall they be your judges. But if I by the Spirit of God cast out demons, then is the kingdom of God come upon you.

"When the strong man fully armed guardeth his own court, his goods are in peace: but when a stronger than he shall come upon him, and overcome him, he taketh from him his whole armor wherein he trusted, and divideth his spoils. He that is not with me is against me; and he that gathereth not with me scattereth.

"Verily I say unto you, All their sins shall be forgiven unto the sons of men, and their blasphemies wherewith soever they shall blaspheme: but whosoever shall blaspheme against the Holy Spirit hath never forgiveness, but is guilty of an eternal sin:" because they said, "He hath an unclean spirit."

"Either make the tree good, and its fruit good; or make the tree corrupt, and its fruit corrupt: for the tree is known by its fruit. Ye offspring of vipers, how can ye, being evil, speak good things? for out of the abundance of the heart the mouth speaketh. The good man out of his good treasure bringeth forth good things: and the evil man out of his evil treasure bringeth forth evil things. And I say unto you, that every idle word that men shall speak, they shall give account thereof in the day of judgment. For by thy words thou shalt be justified, and by thy words thou shalt be condemned."

THE DEMAND FOR A SIGN.

Then certain of the scribes and Pharisees answered him, saying, "Teacher, we would see a sign from thee."

But he answered and said unto them, "An evil and adulterous generation seeketh after a sign; and there shall no sign be given to it but the sign of Jonah the prophet; for even as Jonah became a sign unto the Ninevites, so shall also the Son of man be to this generation. The queen of the south shall rise up in the judgment with the men of this generation, and shall condemn them: for she came from the ends of the earth to hear the wisdom of Solomon; and behold, a greater than Solomon is here. The men of Nineveh shall stand up in the judgment with this generation, and shall condemn it: for they repented at the preaching of Jonah; and behold, a greater than Jonah is here.

"But the unclean spirit, when he is gone out of the man, passeth through waterless places, seeking rest, and findeth it not. Then he saith, 'I will return into my house whence I came out;' and when he is come, he findeth it empty, swept, and garnished. Then goeth he, and taketh with himself seven other spirits more evil than himself, and they enter in and dwell there: and the last state of that man becometh worse than the first. Even so shall it be also unto this evil generation."

And it came to pass, as he said these things, a certain woman out of the multitude lifted up her voice, and said unto him, "Blessed is the womb that bare thee, and the breasts which thou didst suck."

But he said, "Yea rather, blessed are they that hear the word of God and keep it."

THE PARABLES OF THE KINGDOM
THE SOWER.

On that day went Jesus out of the house, and sat by the sea side. And there were gathered unto him great multitudes, so that he entered into a boat, and sat; and all the multitude stood on the beach. And he spake to them many things in parables, saying, "Hearken: Behold, the sower went forth to sow: and it came to pass, as he sowed, some seed fell by the wayside, and the birds came and devoured it. And other fell on the rocky ground, where it had not much earth; and straightway it sprang up, because it had no deepness of earth: and when the sun was risen, it was scorched; and because it had no root, it withered away. And other fell among the thorns, and the thorns grew up, and choked it, and it yielded no fruit. And others fell into the good ground, and yielded fruit, growing up and increasing; and brought forth, thirtyfold, and sixtyfold, and a hundredfold." And he said, "Who hath ears to hear, let him hear."

And when he was alone, they that were about him with the twelve came, and said unto him, "Why speakest thou unto them in parables?"

And he answered and said unto them, "Unto you it is given to know the mysteries of the kingdom of heaven, but to them it is not given. For whosoever hath, to him shall be given, and he shall have abundance: but whosoever hath not, from him shall be taken away even that which he hath. Therefore speak I to them in parables; because seeing they see not, and hearing they hear not, neither do they understand. And unto them is fulfilled the prophecy of Isaiah, which saith,

"'By hearing ye shall hear, and shall in no wise understand;
And seeing ye shall see, and shall in no wise perceive;
For this people's heart is waxed gross,
And their ears are dull of hearing,
And their eyes they have closed;
Lest haply they should perceive with their eyes,
And hear with their ears,
And understand with their heart,
And should turn again,
And I should heal them.'

"But blessed are your eyes, for they see; and your ears, for they hear. For verily I say unto you, that many prophets and righteous men desired to see the things which ye see, and saw them not; and to hear the things which ye hear, and heard them not."

And he saith unto them, "Know ye not this parable? and how, shall ye know all the parables? The sower soweth the word. The seed is the word of God. When any one heareth the word of the kingdom, and understandeth it not, then cometh the evil one, and snatcheth away that which hath been sown in his heart. This is he that was sown by the way side. And he that was sown upon the rocky places, this is he that heareth the word, and straightway with joy receiveth it; yet hath he not root in himself, but endureth for a while; and when tribulation or persecution ariseth because of the word, straightway he stumbleth. And he that was sown among the thorns, this is he that heareth the word; and the care of the world, and the deceitfulness of riches, and the pleasures of this life, choke the word, and he becometh unfruitful. And he that was sown upon the good ground, this is he that heareth the word in an honest and good heart, and understandeth it, who verily beareth fruit, and bringeth forth, some a hundredfold, some sixty, some thirty."

THE TARES.

Another parable set he before them, saying, "The kingdom of heaven is likened unto a man that sowed good seed in his field: but while men slept, his enemy came and sowed tares also among the wheat, and went away. But when the blade sprang up and brought forth fruit, then appeared the tares also. And the servants of the householder came and said unto him, 'Sir, didst thou not sow good seed in thy field? whence then hath it tares?' And he said unto them, 'An enemy hath done this.' And the servants say unto him, 'Wilt thou then that we go and gather them up?' But he saith, 'Nay; lest haply while ye gather up the tares, ye root up the wheat with them. Let both grow together until the harvest: and in the time of the harvest I will say to the reapers, Gather up first the tares, and bind them in bundles to burn them; but gather the wheat into my barn.'"

THE GROWING GRAIN.

And he said, "So is the kingdom of God, as if a man should cast seed upon the earth; and should sleep and rise night and day, and the seed should spring up and grow, he knoweth not how. The earth beareth fruit of herself; first the blade, then the ear, then the full grain in the ear. But when the fruit is ripe, straightway he putteth forth the sickle, because the harvest is come."

THE MUSTARD SEED.

And he said, "How shall we liken the kingdom of God? or in what parable shall we set it forth? It is like a grain of mustard seed, which, when it is sown upon the earth, though it be less than all the seeds that are upon the earth, yet when it is sown, groweth up, and becometh greater than all the herbs, and putteth out great branches; so that the birds of the heaven can lodge under the shadow thereof."

THE LEAVEN.

Another parable spake he unto them: "The kingdom of heaven is like unto leaven, which a woman took, and hid in three measures of meal, till it was all leavened."

THE UNDERSTANDING OF PARABLES.

All these things spake Jesus in parables unto the multitudes; and without a parable spake he nothing unto them: that it might be fulfilled which was spoken through the prophet, saying,

"I will open my mouth in parables;
I will utter things hidden from the foundation of the world."

Then he left the multitudes, and went into the house: and his disciples came unto him, saying, "Explain unto us the parable of the tares of the field."

And he answered and said, "He that soweth the good seed is the Son of man; and the field is the world; and the good seed, these are the sons of the kingdom; and the tares are the sons of the evil one; and the enemy that sowed them is the devil: and the harvest is the end of the world; and the reapers are angels. As therefore the tares are gathered up and burned with fire; so shall it be in the end of the world. The Son of man shall send forth his angels and they shall gather out of his kingdom all things that cause stumbling and them that do iniquity and shall cast them into the furnace of fire: there shall be the weeping and the gnashing of teeth. Then shall the righteous shine forth as the sun in the kingdom of their Father. He that hath ears let him hear."

THE HID TREASURE.

"The kingdom of heaven is like unto a treasure hidden in the field; which a man found, and hid; and in his joy he goeth and selleth all that he hath, and buyeth that field."

THE PEARL OF GREAT PRICE.

"Again, the kingdom of heaven is like unto a man that is a merchant seeking goodly pearls: and having found one pearl of great price, he went and sold all that he had, and bought it."

THE DRAG NET.

"Again, the kingdom of heaven is like unto a net, that was cast into the sea, and gathered of every kind: which, when it was filled, they drew up on the beach; and they sat down, and gathered the good into vessels, but the bad they cast away. So shall it be in the end of the world: the angels shall come forth, and sever the wicked from among the righteous, and shall cast them into the furnace of fire: there shall be the weeping and the gnashing of teeth.

"Have ye understood all these things?"

They say unto him, "Yea."

And he said unto them, "Therefore every scribe who hath been made a disciple to the kingdom of heaven is like unto a man that is a householder, who bringeth forth out of his treasure things new and old."

A DAY OF MIRACLES BY THE LAKE
JESUS STILLS THE STORM.

And on that day, when even was come, he saith unto them, "Let us go over unto the other side."

And leaving the multitude, they take him with them, even as he was, in the boat. And other boats were with him. And there ariseth a great storm of wind, and the waves beat into the boat, insomuch that the boat was now filling. And he himself was in the stern, asleep on the cushion: and they awake him, and say unto him, "Save, Lord; we perish."

And he awoke, and rebuked the wind, and said unto the sea, "Peace, be still."

And the wind ceased, and there was a great calm. And he said unto them, "Why are ye fearful? have ye not yet faith?"

And they feared exceedingly, and said one to another, "Who then is this, that even the wind and the sea obey him?"

THE LEGION OF DEMONS.

And they arrived at the country of the Gerasenes, which is over against Galilee. And when he was come forth upon the land, there met him a certain man out of the city, who had demons; and for a long time he had worn no clothes, and abode not in any house, but in the tombs.

And when he saw Jesus, he cried out, and fell down before him, and with a loud voice said, "What have I to do with thee, Jesus, thou Son of the Most High God? I beseech thee, torment me not." For he was commanding the unclean spirit to come out from the man. For oftentimes it had seized him; and he was kept under guard, and bound with chains and fetters; and breaking the bands asunder, he was driven of the demon into the deserts.

And Jesus asked him, "What is thy name?"

And he said, "Legion;" for many demons were entered into him.

And they entreated him that he would not command them to depart into the abyss. Now there was there a herd of many swine feeding on the mountain. And the demons besought him, saying, "If thou cast us out, send us away into the herd of swine."

And he said unto them, "Go."

And they came out, and went into the swine: and behold, the whole herd rushed down the steep into the sea, in number about two thousand; and they were drowned in the sea.

And they that fed them fled, and told it in the city, and in the country. And they came to see what it was that had come to pass. And they come to Jesus, and behold him that was possessed with demons sitting, clothed and in his right mind, even him that had the legion: and they were afraid. And they that saw it declared unto them how it befell him that was possessed with demons, and concerning the swine. And they began to beseech him to depart from them; for they were holden with great fear.

And as he was entering into the boat, he that had been possessed with demons besought him that he might be with him. And he suffered him not, but saith unto him, "Go to thy house unto thy friends, and tell them how great things the Lord hath done for thee, and how he had mercy on thee."

And he went his way, and began to publish in Decapolis how great things Jesus had done for him: and all men marvelled.

THE DYING CHILD AND THE SUFFERING WOM AN.

And when Jesus had crossed over again in the boat unto the other side, the multitude welcomed him; for they were all waiting for him; and he was by the sea.

And there cometh one of the rulers of the synagogue, Jairus by name; and seeing him, he falleth at his feet, and beseecheth him much, saying, "My little daughter is at the point of death: I pray thee, that thou come and lay thy hands on her, that she may be made whole, and live."

And he went with him; and a great multitude followed him, and they thronged him.

And a woman, who had an issue of blood twelve years, and had suffered many things of many physicians, and had spent all that she had, and was nothing bettered, but rather grew worse, having heard the things concerning Jesus, came in the crowd behind, and touched the border of his garment. For she said, "If I touch but his garments, I shall be made whole." And straightway the fountain of her blood was dried up; and she felt in her body that she was healed of her plague.

And straightway Jesus, perceiving in himself that the power proceeding from him had gone forth, turned him about in the crowd, and said, "Who touched my garments?"

And when all denied, Peter said, and they that were with him, "Master, the multitudes press thee and crush thee, and sayest thou, 'Who touched me?'"

But Jesus said, "Some one did touch me; for I perceived that power had gone forth from me."

And he looked round about to see her that had done this thing. And when the woman saw that she was not hid, she came trembling, and falling down before him declared in the presence of all the people for what cause she touched him, and how she was healed immediately.

And he said unto her, "Daughter, thy faith hath made thee whole; go in peace, and be whole of thy plague."

While he yet spake, they come from the ruler of the synagogue's house, saying, "Thy daughter is dead: why troublest thou the Teacher any further?"

But Jesus, not heeding the word spoken, saith unto the ruler of the synagogue, "Fear not: only believe, and she shall be made whole."

And he suffered no man to follow with him, save Peter, and James, and John the brother of James. And when Jesus came into the ruler's house, and saw the flute-players, and the crowd making a tumult, and many weeping and wailing greatly, he said, "Give place: why make ye a tumult and weep? the child is not dead, but sleepeth."

And they laughed him to scorn, knowing that she was dead. But he, having put them all forth, taketh the father of the child and her mother and them that were with him, and goeth in where the child was. And taking the child by the hand, he saith unto her. "Talitha cumi;" which is, being interpreted, "Damsel, I say unto thee, Arise."

And her spirit returned. And straightway the damsel rose up, and walked: for she was twelve years old. And they were amazed straightway with a great amazement. And he charged them much that no man should know this: and he commanded that something should be given her to eat.

And the fame hereof went forth into all that land.

HEALINGS BY THE WAY.

And as Jesus passed by from thence, two blind men followed him, crying out, and saying, "Have mercy on us, thou son of David."

And when he was come into the house, the blind men came to him: and Jesus saith unto them, "Believe ye that I am able to do this?"

They say unto him, "Yea, Lord."

Then touched he their eyes, saying, "According to your faith be it done unto you."

And their eyes were opened. And Jesus strictly charged them, saying, "See that no man know it."

But they went forth, and spread abroad his fame in all that land.

And as they went forth, behold, there was brought to him a dumb man possessed with a demon. And when the demon was cast out, the dumb man spake: and the multitudes marvelled, saying, "It was never so seen in Israel."

But the Pharisees said, "By the prince of the demons casteth he out demons."

WIDER EVANGELIZATION OF GALILEE
A VISIT TO HIS HOME.

And he went out from thence; and he cometh into his own country to Nazareth, where he had been brought up; and his disciples follow him. And when the sabbath was come, he entered, as his custom was, into the synagogue, and stood up to read. And there was delivered unto him the book of the prophet Isaiah. And he opened the book, and found the place where it was written,

"The Spirit of the Lord is upon me, Because he anointed me to preach good tidings to the poor; He hath sent me to proclaim release to the captives, And recovering of sight to the blind, To set at liberty them that are bruised, To proclaim the acceptable year of the Lord."

And he closed the book, and gave it back to the attendant, and sat down: and the eyes of all in the synagogue were fastened on him.

And he began to say unto them, "To-day hath this scripture been fulfilled in your ears."

And all bare him witness, and wondered at the words of grace which proceeded out of his mouth: and they said, "Whence hath this man these things?" and, "What is the wisdom that is given unto this man, and what mean such mighty works wrought by his hands? Is not this the carpenter, the son of Mary, and brother of James, and Joses, and Judas, and Simon? and are not his sisters here with us?" And they were offended in him.

And he said unto them, "Doubtless ye will say unto me this parable, Physician, heal thyself: whatsoever we have heard done at Capernaum, do also here in thine own country."

And he said, "Verily I say unto you, A prophet is not without honor, save in his own country, and among his own kin, and in his own house. But of a truth I say unto you, There were many widows in Israel in the days of Elijah, when the heaven was shut up three years and six months, when there came a great famine over all the land; and unto none of them was Elijah sent, but only to Zarephath, in the land of Sidon, unto a woman that was a widow. And there were many lepers in Israel in the time of Elisha the prophet; and none of them was cleansed, but only Naaman the Syrian."

And they were all filled with wrath in the synagogue, as they heard these things; and they rose up, and cast him forth out of the city, and led him unto the brow of the hill whereon their city was built, that they might throw him down headlong. But he passing through the midst of them went his way.

And he could there do no mighty work, save that he laid his hands upon a few sick folk, and healed them.

PREACHING IN THE VILLAGES.

And Jesus went about all the cities and the villages, teaching in their synagogues, and preaching the gospel of the kingdom, and healing all manner of disease and all manner of sickness. But when he saw the multitudes, he was moved with compassion for them, because they were distressed and scattered, as sheep not having a shepherd.

Then saith he unto his disciples, "The harvest indeed is plenteous, but the laborers are few. Pray ye therefore the Lord of the harvest, that he send forth laborers into his harvest."

THE TWELVE SENT FORTH.

And he calleth unto him his twelve disciples, and began to send them forth by two and two; and he gave them power and authority over unclean spirits, to cast them out, and to heal all manner of disease and all manner of sickness.

And he charged them, saying, "Go not into any way of the Gentiles, and enter not into any city of the Samaritans: but go rather to the lost sheep of the house of Israel. And as ye go, preach, saying, 'The kingdom of heaven is at hand.' Heal the sick, raise the dead, cleanse the lepers, cast out demons: freely ye received, freely give.

"Get you no gold, nor silver, nor brass in your purses. Take nothing for your journey, save a staff only; no bread, no wallet; neither have two coats, nor shoes, but go shod with sandals: for the laborer is worthy of his food. And into whatsoever city or village ye shall enter, search out who in it is worthy; and there abide till ye go forth. And as ye enter into the house, salute it. And if the house be worthy, let your peace come upon it: but if it be not worthy, let your peace return to you. And whosoever shall not receive you, nor hear your words, as ye go forth out of that house or that city, shake off the dust from your feet for a testimony against them. Verily I say unto you, It shall be more tolerable for the land of Sodom and Gomorrah in the day of judgment, than for that city.

"Behold, I send you forth as sheep in the midst of wolves: be ye therefore wise as serpents, and harmless as doves. But beware of men: for they will deliver you up to councils, and in their synagogues they will scourge you; yea and before governors and kings shall ye be brought for my sake, for a testimony to them and to the Gentiles. But when they deliver you up, be not anxious how or what ye shall speak: for it shall be given you in that hour what ye shall speak. For it is not ye that speak, but the Spirit of your Father that speaketh in you. And brother shall deliver up brother to death, and the father his child: and children shall rise up against parents, and cause them to be put to death. And ye shall be hated of all men, for my name's sake: but he that endureth to the end, the same shall be saved. But when they persecute you in this city, flee into the next: for verily I say unto you, Ye shall not have gone through the cities of Israel, till the Son of man be come.

"A disciple is not above his teacher, nor a servant above his lord. It is enough for the disciple that he be as his teacher, and the servant as his lord. If they have called the master of the house Beelzebub, how much more them of his household? Fear them not therefore: for there is nothing covered, that shall not be revealed; and hid, that shall not be known. What I tell you in the darkness, speak ye in the light; and what ye hear in the ear, proclaim upon the house-tops. And be not afraid of them that kill the body, but are not able to kill the soul: but rather fear him who is able to destroy both soul and body in hell. Are not two sparrows sold for a penny? and not one of them shall fall on the ground without your Father: but the very hairs of your head are all numbered. Fear not therefore: ye are of more value than many sparrows. Every one therefore who shall confess me before men, him will I also confess before my Father who is in heaven. But whosoever shall deny me before men, him will I also deny before my Father who is in heaven.

"I came to cast fire upon the earth; and what do I desire, if it is already kindled? But I have a baptism to be baptized with; and how am I straitened till it be accomplished!

"Think not that I came to send peace on the earth: I came not to send peace, but a sword. For there shall be from henceforth five in one house divided, three against two, and two against three. For I came to set a man at variance against his father, and the daughter against her mother, and the daughter in law against her mother in law: and a man's foes shall be they of his own household. He that loveth father or mother more than me is not worthy of me; and he that loveth son or daughter more than me is not worthy of me. And he that doth not take his cross and follow after me, is not worthy of me. He that findeth his life shall lose it; and he that loseth his life for my sake shall find it.

"He that receiveth you receiveth me, and he that receiveth me receiveth him that sent me. He that receiveth a prophet in the name of a prophet shall receive a prophet's reward: and he that receiveth a righteous man in the name of a righteous man shall receive a righteous man's reward. And whosoever shall give to drink unto one of these little ones a cup of cold water only, in the name of a disciple, verily I say unto you he shall in no wise lose his reward."

And they departed, and went throughout the villages, preaching the gospel, and healing everywhere.

And they cast out many demons, and anointed with oil many that were sick, and healed them.

And Jesus departed thence to teach and preach. And wheresoever he entered, into villages, or into cities, or into the country, they laid the sick in the marketplaces, and besought him that they might touch if it were but the border of his garment: and as many as touched him were made whole.

At that season Herod the tetrarch heard the report concerning Jesus, and said unto his servants, "This is John the Baptist; he is risen from the dead; and therefore do these powers work in him."

But others said, "It is Elijah." And others said, "It is a prophet, even as one of the prophets."

But Herod, when he heard thereof, said, "John, whom I beheaded, he is risen."

And he sought to see him.

THE CRISIS IN CAPERNAUM
THE FIVE THOUSAND FED.

And the apostles, when they were returned unto Jesus, told him all things, whatsoever they had done, and whatsoever they had taught.

Now the passover, the feast of the Jews, was at hand. And he saith unto them, "Come ye yourselves apart into a desert place, and rest a while." For there were many coming and going, and they had no leisure so much as to eat.

And they went away in the boat to a desert place apart. And the people saw them going, and many knew them, and they ran together there on foot from all the cities, and outwent them.

And he came forth and saw a great multitude. And he welcomed them, and spake to them of the kingdom of God, and them that had need of healing he cured. And he had compassion on them, because they were as sheep not having a shepherd.

And the day began to wear away; and the twelve came, and said unto him, "Send the multitude away, that they may go into the villages and country round about, and lodge, and get provisions: for we are here in a desert place."

But Jesus said unto them, "They have no need to go away: give ye them to eat."

Philip answered him, "Two hundred shillings' worth of bread is not sufficient for them, that every one may take a little."

Jesus saith unto them, "How many loaves have ye? go and see."

One of his disciples, Andrew, Simon Peter's brother, saith unto him, "There is a lad here, who hath five barley loaves, and two fishes: but what are these among so many?"

And Jesus said, "Bring them hither to me."

And he commanded them that all should sit down by companies upon the green grass. Now there was much grass in the place. And they sat down in ranks, by hundreds, and by fifties. And he took the five loaves and the two fishes, and looking up to heaven, he blessed, and brake the loaves; and he gave to the disciples to set before them; and the two fishes divided he among them all. And they all ate, and were filled. And they took up broken pieces, twelve basketfuls, and also of the fishes. And they that ate the loaves were five thousand men.

When therefore the people saw the sign which he did, they said, "This is of a truth the prophet that cometh into the world."

Jesus therefore perceiving that they were about to come and take him by force, to make him king, constrained the disciples to enter into the boat, and to go before him unto the other side, till he should send the multitudes away.

And after he had sent the multitudes away, he went up into the mountain apart to pray: and when even was come, he was there alone.

JESUS WALKING ON THE WATER.

And his disciples were going over the sea unto Capernaum. And it was now dark, and Jesus had not yet come to them. And the sea was rising by reason of a great wind that blew. And in the fourth watch of the night, when they had rowed about five and twenty or thirty furlongs, they behold Jesus walking on the sea, and drawing nigh unto the boat. And when the disciples saw him walking on the sea, they were troubled, saying, "It is a ghost;" and they cried out for fear.

But straightway Jesus spake unto them, saying, "Be of good cheer; it is I; be not afraid."

And Peter answered him and said, "Lord, if it be thou, bid me come unto thee upon the waters."

And he said, "Come."

And Peter went down from the boat, and walked upon the waters, to come to Jesus. But when he saw the wind, he was afraid; and beginning to sink, he cried out, saying, "Lord, save me."

And immediately Jesus stretched forth his hand, and took hold of him, and saith unto him, "O thou of little faith, wherefore didst thou doubt?"

And when they were gone up into the boat, the wind ceased: and they were sore amazed in themselves; for they understood not concerning the loaves, but their heart was hardened.

And when they had crossed over, they came to the land unto Gennesaret, and moored to the shore. And when they were come out of the boat, straightway the people knew him, and ran round about that whole region, and began to carry about on their beds those that were sick, where they heard he was.

THE DISAPPOINTMENT OF THE PEOPLE.

On the morrow the multitude that stood on the other side of the sea saw that there was no other boat there, save one, and that Jesus entered not with his disciples into the boat, but that his disciples went away alone (howbeit there came boats from Tiberias nigh unto the place where they ate the bread after the Lord had given thanks): when the multitude therefore saw that Jesus was not there, neither his disciples, they themselves got into the boats, and came to Capernaum, seeking Jesus.

And when they found him on the other side of the sea, they said unto him, "Rabbi, when camest thou hither?"

Jesus answered them and said, "Verily, verily, I say unto you, Ye seek me, not because ye saw signs, but because ye ate of the loaves, and were filled. Work not for the food which perisheth, but for the food which abideth unto eternal life, which the Son of man shall give unto you; for him the Father, even God, hath sealed."

They said therefore unto him, "What must we do, that we may work the works of God?"

Jesus answered and said unto them, "This is the work of God, that ye believe on him whom he hath sent."

They said therefore unto him, "What then doest thou for a sign, that we may see, and believe thee? what workest thou? Our fathers ate the manna in the wilderness; as it is written, 'He gave them bread out of heaven to eat.'"

Jesus therefore said unto them, "Verily, verily, I say unto you, It was not Moses that gave you the bread out of heaven; but my Father giveth you the true bread out of heaven. For the bread of God is that which cometh down out of heaven, and giveth life unto the world."

They said therefore unto him, "Lord, evermore give us this bread."

Jesus said unto them, "I am the bread of life: he that cometh to me shall not hunger, and he that believeth on me shall never thirst. But I said unto you, that ye have seen me, and yet believe not. All that which the Father giveth me shall come unto me; and him that cometh to me I will in no wise cast out. For I am come down from heaven, not to do mine own will, but the will of him that sent me. And this is the will of him that sent me, that of all that which he hath given me I should lose nothing, but should raise it up at the last day. For this is the will of my Father, that every one that beholdeth the Son, and believeth on him, should have eternal life; and I will raise him up at the last day."

The Jews therefore murmured concerning him, because he said, "I am the bread which came down out of heaven." And they said, "Is not this Jesus, the son of Joseph, whose father and mother we know? how doth he now say 'I am come down out of heaven'?"

Jesus answered and said unto them, "Murmur not among yourselves. No man can come to me, except the Father that sent me draw him: and I will raise him up in the last day. It is written in the prophets, 'And they shall all be taught of God.' Every one that hath heard from the Father, and hath learned, cometh unto me. Not that any man hath seen the Father, save he that is from God, he hath seen the Father. Verily, verily, I say unto you, He that believeth hath eternal life. I am the bread of life. Your fathers ate the manna in the wilderness, and they died. This is the bread which cometh down out of heaven, that a man may eat thereof, and not die. I am the living bread which came down out of heaven: if any man eat of this bread, he shall live for ever: yea and the bread which I will give is my flesh, for the life of the world."

The Jews therefore strove one with another, saying, "How can this man give us his flesh to eat?"

Jesus therefore said unto them, "Verily, verily, I say unto you, Except ye eat the flesh of the Son of man and drink his blood, ye have not life in yourselves. He that eateth my flesh and drinketh my blood hath eternal life; and I will raise him up at the last day. For my flesh is meat indeed, and my blood is drink indeed. He that eateth my flesh and drinketh my blood abideth in me, and I in him. As the living Father sent me, and I live because of the Father; so he that eateth me, he also shall live because of me. This is the bread which came down out of heaven: not as the fathers ate, and died; he that eateth this bread shall live for ever."

These things said he in the synagogue, as he taught in Capernaum.

Many therefore of his disciples, when they heard this, said, "This is a hard saying; who can hear it?"

But Jesus knowing in himself that his disciples murmured at this, said unto them, "Doth this cause you to stumble? What then if ye should behold the Son of man ascending where he was before? It is the spirit that giveth life; the flesh profiteth nothing: the words that I have spoken unto you are spirit, and are life. But there are some of you that believe not."

For Jesus knew from the beginning who they were that believed not, and who it was that should betray him. And he said, "For this cause have I said unto you, that no man can come unto me, except it be given unto him of the Father."

Upon this many of his disciples went back, and walked no more with him. Jesus said therefore unto the twelve, "Would ye also go away?"

Simon Peter answered him, "Lord, to whom shall we go? thou hast the words of eternal life. And we have believed and know that thou art the Holy One of God."

Jesus answered them, "Did not I choose you the twelve, and one of you is a devil?"

Now he spake of Judas, the son of Simon Iscariot, for he it was that should betray him, being one of the twelve.

REJECTION OF THE TRADITION OF THE ELDERS.

And there are gathered together unto him the Pharisees, and certain of the scribes, who had come from Jerusalem, and had seen that some of his disciples ate their bread with defiled, that is, unwashen, hands. (For the Pharisees, and all the Jews, except they wash their hands diligently, eat not, holding the tradition of the elders; and when they come from the market-place, except they bathe themselves, they eat not; and many other things there are, which they have received to hold, washings of cups, and pots, and brasen vessels.) And the Pharisees and the scribes ask him, "Why walk not thy disciples according to the tradition of the elders, but eat their bread with defiled hands?"

And he said unto them, "Well did Isaiah prophesy of you hypocrites, as it is written,

> 'This people honoreth me with their lips,
> But their heart is far from me.
> But in vain do they worship me,
> Teaching as their doctrines the precepts of men.'

"Ye leave the commandment of God, and hold fast the tradition of men."

And he said unto them, "Full well do ye reject the commandment of God, that ye may keep your tradition. For Moses said, 'Honor thy father and thy mother;' and, 'He that speaketh evil of father or mother, let him die the death;' but ye say, 'If a man shall say to his father or his mother, That wherewith thou mightest have been profited by me is Corban,' that is to say, Given to God; ye no longer suffer him to do aught for his father or his mother; making void the word of God by your tradition, which ye have delivered: and many such like things ye do."

And he called to him the multitude again, and said unto them, "Hear me all of you, and understand: there is nothing from without the man, that going into him can defile him; but the things which proceed out of the man are those that defile the man."

Then came the disciples, and said unto him, "Knowest thou that the Pharisees were offended, when they heard this saying?"

But he answered and said, "Every plant which my heavenly Father planted not, shall be rooted up. Let them alone: they are blind guides. And if the blind guide the blind, both shall fall into a pit."

And when he was entered into the house from the multitude, his disciples asked of him the parable.

And he saith unto them, "Are ye also even yet without understanding? Perceive ye not, that whatsoever from without goeth into the man, it cannot defile him; because it goeth not into his heart, but into his belly, and goeth out into the draught?"

This he said, making all meats clean. And he said, "That which proceedeth out of the man, that defileth the man. For from within, out of the heart of men, evil thoughts proceed, fornications, thefts, murders, adulteries, covetings, wickedness, deceit, false witness, lasciviousness, an evil eye, railing, pride, foolishness: all these evil things proceed from within, and defile the man; but to eat with unwashen hands defileth not the man."

THE PLOT OF THE PHARISEES.

And it came to pass on a sabbath, that he entered into the synagogue and taught: and there was a man there, and his right hand was withered. And the scribes and the Pharisees watched him, whether he would heal on the sabbath; that they might find how to accuse him. But he knew their thoughts; and he said to the man that had his hand withered, "Rise up, and stand forth in the midst."

And he arose and stood forth. And Jesus said unto them, "I ask you, Is it lawful on the sabbath to do good, or to do harm? to save a life or to destroy it? What man shall there be of you, that shall have one sheep, and if this fall into a pit on the sabbath day, will he not lay hold on it, and lift it out? How much then is a man of more value than a sheep! Wherefore it is lawful to do good on the sabbath day."

But they held their peace. And when he had looked round about on them with anger, being grieved at the hardening of their heart, he saith unto the man, "Stretch forth thy hand."

And he stretched it forth; and his hand was restored whole, as the other.

But they were filled with madness; and communed one with another what they might do to Jesus.

And the Pharisees went out, and straightway with the Herodians took counsel against him, how they might destroy him.

=HIS WITHDRAWAL WITH THE TWELVE=

THE MINISTRY BEYOND GALILEE
THE PHOENICIAN RETIREMENT
AND THE GENTILE CURE.

And Jesus went out thence, and withdrew into the parts of Tyre and Sidon.

And he entered into a house, and would have no man know it; and he could not be hid. But straightway a woman, whose little daughter had an unclean spirit, having heard of him, came and fell down at his feet. Now the woman was a Greek, a Syrophoenician by race.

And she cried, saying, "Have mercy on me, O Lord, thou son of David; my daughter is grievously vexed with a demon."

But he answered her not a word. And his disciples came and besought him, saying, "Send her away, for she crieth after us."

But he answered and said, "I was not sent but unto the lost sheep of the house of Israel."

But she came and worshipped him, saying, "Lord help me."

And he said unto her, "Let the children first be filled: for it is not meet to take the children's bread and cast it to the dogs."

But she answered and saith unto him, "Yea, Lord; even the dogs under the table eat of the children's crumbs."

Then Jesus answered and said unto her, "O woman, great is thy faith: be it done unto thee as thou wilt. Go thy way; the demon is gone out of thy daughter."

And she went away unto her house, and found the child laid upon the bed, and the demon gone out.

MIRACLES AND MULTITUDES AGAIN.

And again he went out from the borders of Tyre, and came through Sidon unto the sea of Galilee, through the midst of the borders of Decapolis.

And he went up into the mountain, and sat there. And there came unto him great multitudes, having with them the lame, blind, dumb, maimed, and many others, and they cast them down at his feet; and he healed them; insomuch that the multitude wondered, when they saw the dumb speaking, the maimed whole, and the lame walking, and the blind seeing; and they glorified the God of Israel.

And they bring unto him one that was deaf, and had an impediment in his speech; and they beseech him to lay his hand upon him. And he took him aside from the multitude privately, and put his fingers into his ears, and he spat, and touched his tongue; and looking up to heaven, he sighed, and saith unto him, "Ephphatha," that is, "Be opened."

And his ears were opened, and the bond of his tongue was loosed, and he spake plain. And he charged them that they should tell no man; but the more he charged them, so much the more a great deal they published it. And they were beyond measure astonished, saying, "He hath done all things well; he maketh even the deaf to hear, and the dumb to speak."

THE FOUR THOUSAND FED.

In those days, when there was again a great multitude, and they had nothing to eat, he called unto him his disciples, and saith unto them, "I have compassion on the multitude, because they continue with me now three days, and have nothing to eat; and if I send them away fasting to their home, they will faint on the way; and some of them are come from far."

And his disciples answered him, "Whence shall one be able to fill these men with bread here in a desert place?"

And he asked them, "How many loaves have ye?"

And they said, "Seven."

And he commandeth the multitude to sit down on the ground: and he took the seven loaves, and having given thanks, he brake, and gave to his disciples, to set before them; and they set them before the multitude.

And they had a few small fishes: and having blessed them, he commanded to set these also before them. And they ate and were filled: and they took up, of broken pieces that remained over, seven baskets. And they were about four thousand men, besides women and children.

And he sent away the multitudes, and entered into the boat, and came into the borders of Magadan.

THE PHARISEES AND SADUCCEES DEMAND A SIGN.

And the Pharisees and Sadducees came forth, and began to question with him, seeking of him a sign from heaven, trying him.

But he answered and said unto them, "When it is evening, ye say, 'It will be fair weather,' for the heaven is red. And in the morning, 'It will be foul weather to-day,' for the heaven is red and lowering. Ye know how to discern the face of the heaven; but ye cannot discern the signs of the times."

And he sighed deeply in his spirit, and saith. "Why doth this generation seek a sign? verily I say unto you, There shall no sign be given unto this generation."

And he left them, and again entering into the boat departed to the other side.

And they forgot to take bread; and they had not in the boat with them more than one loaf. And he charged them, saying, "Take heed, beware of the leaven of the Pharisees and the leaven of Herod."

And they reasoned one with another, saying, "We have no bread."

And Jesus perceiving it saith unto them, "O ye of little faith, why reason ye among yourselves, because ye have no bread? Do ye not yet perceive, neither understand? have ye your heart hardened? Having eyes, see ye not? and having ears, hear ye not? and do ye not remember? When I brake the five loaves among the five thousand, how many baskets full of broken pieces took ye up?"

They say unto him, "Twelve."

"And when the seven among the four thousand, how many basketfuls of broken pieces took ye up?"

And they say unto him, "Seven."

And he said unto them, "How is it that ye do not perceive that I spake not to you concerning bread? But beware of the leaven of the Pharisees and Sadducees."

Then understood they that he bade them not beware of the leaven of bread, but of the teaching of the Pharisees and Sadducees.

THE BLIND MAN HEALED.

And they come unto Bethsaida. And they bring to him a blind man, and beseech him to touch him. And he took hold of the blind man by the hand, and brought him out of the village; and when he had spit on his eyes, and laid his hands upon him, he asked him, "Seest thou aught?"

And he looked up, and said, "I see men; for I behold them as trees, walking."

Then again he laid his hands upon his eyes; and he looked stedfastly, and was restored, and saw all things clearly. And he sent him away to his home, saying, "Do not even enter into the village."

JESUS THE MESSIAH
PETER'S CONFESSION.

And Jesus went forth, and his disciples, into the villages of Caesarea Philippi.

And it came to pass, as he was praying apart, the disciples were with him: and he asked them, saying, "Who do the multitudes say that I am?"

And they answering, said, "Some say John the Baptist; some Elijah; and others, Jeremiah; and others, that one of the old prophets is risen again."

And he said unto them, "But who say ye that I am?"

And Simon Peter answered and said, "Thou art the Christ, the Son of the living God."

And Jesus answered and said unto him, "Blessed art thou, Simon Bar-Jonah: for flesh and blood hath not revealed it unto thee, but my Father who is in heaven. And I also say unto thee, that thou art Peter, and upon this rock I will build my church; and the gates of Hades shall not prevail against it. I will give unto thee the keys of the kingdom of heaven: and whatsoever thou shalt bind on earth shall be bound in heaven; and whatsoever thou shalt loose on earth shall be loosed in heaven."

Then charged he the disciples that they should tell no man that he was the Christ.

THE PASSION AND RESURRECTION FORETOLD.

From that time began Jesus to show unto his disciples, that he must go unto Jerusalem, and suffer many things and be rejected by the elders, and the chief priests, and the scribes, and be killed, and after three days rise again. And he spake the saying openly.

And Peter took him, and began to rebuke him, saying, "Be it far from thee, Lord: this shall never be unto thee."

But he turning about, and seeing his disciples, rebuked Peter, and saith, "Get thee behind me, Satan: thou art a stumbling-block unto me: for thou mindest not the things of God, but the things of men."

And he called unto him the multitude with his disciples, and said unto them, "If any man would come after me, let him deny himself, and take up his cross daily, and follow me. For whosoever would save his life shall lose it; and whosoever shall lose his life for my sake and the gospel's shall save it. For what doth it profit a man to gain the whole world, and forfeit his life? For what should a man give in exchange for his life? For whosoever shall be ashamed of me and of my words in this adulterous and sinful generation, the Son of man also shall be ashamed of him, when he cometh in his own glory, and the glory of the Father, and of the holy angels. But I tell you of a truth, There are some of them that stand here, who shall in no wise taste of death, till they see the kingdom of God come with power."

THE TRANSFIGURATION.

And it came to pass about eight days after these sayings, that he took with him Peter and John and James, and went up into the mountain to pray. And as he was praying he was transfigured before them; and his face did shine as the sun, and his garments became glistering, white as the light, so as no fuller on earth can whiten them.

And behold, there talked with him two men, who were Moses and Elijah; who appeared in glory, and spake of his decease which he was about to accomplish at Jerusalem.

Now Peter and they that were with him were heavy with sleep; but when they were fully awake, they saw his glory, and the two men that stood with him. And it came to pass, as they were parting from him, Peter said unto Jesus, "Master, it is good for us to be here: and let us make three tabernacles; one for thee, and one for Moses, and one for Elijah:" not knowing what he said.

While he was yet speaking, behold, a bright cloud overshadowed them: and they feared as they entered into the cloud.

And behold, a voice out of the cloud, saying, "This is my beloved Son, in whom I am well pleased; hear ye him."

And when the disciples heard it, they fell on their face, and were sore afraid. And Jesus came and touched them and said, "Arise, and be not afraid."

And suddenly looking round about, they saw no one any more, save Jesus only with themselves.

And as they were coming down from the mountain, he charged them that they should tell no man what things they had seen, save when the Son of man should have risen again from the dead.

And they kept the saying, questioning among themselves what the rising again from the dead should mean. And they asked him, saying, "How is it that the scribes say that Elijah must first come?"

And he said unto them, "Elijah indeed cometh first, and restoreth all things: and how is it written of the Son of man, that he should suffer many things and be set at nought? But I say unto you, that Elijah is come, and they have also done unto him whatsoever they would even as it is written of them."

Then understood the disciples that he spake unto them of John the Baptist.

THE EPILEPTIC BOY.

And when they came to the disciples, they saw a great multitude about them, and scribes questioning with them. And straightway all the multitude, when they saw him, were greatly amazed, and running to him saluted him. And he asked them, "What question ye with them?"

And one of the multitude came to him kneeling, and saying, "Teacher, I beseech thee to look upon my son: for he is mine only child: and behold, he hath a dumb spirit; and wheresoever it taketh him, it dasheth him down: and he foameth, and grindeth his teeth, and pineth away: for he is epileptic, and suffereth grievously; for oft-times he falleth into the fire, and oft-times into the water. And I brought him to thy disciples, and they could not cure him."

And Jesus answered and said, "O faithless and perverse generation, how long shall I be with you? how long shall I bear with you? Bring hither thy son."

And they brought him unto him: and when he saw him, straightway the spirit tare him grievously; and he fell on the ground, and wallowed foaming.

And he asked his father, "How long time is it since this hath come unto him?"

And he said, "From a child. And oft-times it hath cast him both into the fire and into the waters, to destroy him: but if thou canst do anything, have compassion on us, and help us."

And Jesus said unto him, "If thou canst! All things are possible to him that believeth."

Straightway the father of the child cried out and said, "I believe; help thou mine unbelief."

And when Jesus saw that a multitude came running together, he rebuked the unclean spirit, saying unto him, "Thou dumb and deaf spirit, I command thee, come out of him, and enter no more into him."

And having cried out, and torn him much, he came out: and the boy became as one dead; insomuch that the more part said, "He is dead."

But Jesus took him by the hand, and raised him up; and he arose, and Jesus gave him back to his father. And they were all astonished at the majesty of God.

And when he was come into the house, his disciples asked him privately, "How is it that we could not cast it out?"

And he said unto them, "This kind can come out by nothing, save by prayer. Verily I say unto you, If ye have faith as a grain of mustard seed, ye shall say unto this mountain, 'Remove hence to yonder place,' and it shall remove; and nothing shall be impossible unto you."

THE TRAINING OF THE TWELVE
THE PASSION AND RESURRECTION
AGAIN FORETOLD.

And they went forth from thence, and passed through Galilee; and he would not that any man should know it. For he taught his disciples, and said unto them, "Let these words sink into your ears: for the Son of man shall be delivered up into the hands of men, and they shall kill him; and when he is killed, after three days he shall rise again."

But they understood not the saying, and were afraid to ask him.

THE GREATEST DISCIPLE.

And they came to Capernaum: and when he was in the house he asked them, "What were ye reasoning on the way?"

But they held their peace: for they had disputed one with another on the way, who was the greatest.

And he sat down, and called the twelve; and he said unto them, "If any man would be first, he shall be last of all, and servant of all."

And he took a little child, and set him in the midst of them: and taking him in his arms, he said unto them, "Verily I say unto you, Except ye turn, and become as little children, ye shall in no wise enter into the kingdom of heaven. Whosoever therefore shall humble himself as this little child, the same is the greatest in the kingdom of heaven. And whoso shall receive one such little child in my name receiveth me: and whosoever receiveth me, receiveth not me, but him that sent me."

John said unto him, "Teacher, we saw one casting out demons in thy name; and we forbade him, because he followed not us."

But Jesus said, "Forbid him not: for there is no man who shall do a mighty work in my name, and be able quickly to speak evil of me. For he that is not against us is for us. For whosoever shall give you a cup of water to drink, because ye are Christ's, verily I say unto you, he shall in no wise lose his reward. But whoso shall cause one of these little ones that believe on me to stumble, it is profitable for him that a great mill-stone should be hanged about his neck, and that he should be sunk in the depth of the sea.

"Woe unto the world because of occasions of stumbling! for it must needs be that the occasions come; but woe to that man through whom the occasion cometh! And if thy hand or thy foot causeth thee to stumble, cut it off, and cast it from thee: it is good for thee to enter into life maimed or halt, rather than having two hands or two feet to be cast into the eternal fire. And if thine eye causeth thee to stumble, pluck it out, and cast it from thee: it is good for thee to enter into life with one eye, rather than having two eyes to be cast into the hell of fire, where their worm dieth not, and the fire is not quenched. For every one shall be salted with fire. Salt is good; but if the salt have lost its saltness, wherewith will ye season it? Have salt in yourselves, and be at peace one with another.

"See that ye despise not one of these little ones: for I say unto you, that in heaven their angels do always behold the face of my Father who is in heaven. How think ye? if any man have a hundred sheep, and one of them be gone astray, doth he not leave the ninety and nine, and go unto the mountains, and seek that which goeth astray? And if so be that he find it, verily I say unto you, he rejoiceth over it more than over the ninety and nine which have not gone astray. Even so it is not the will of your Father who is in heaven, that one of these little ones should perish.

FORGIVENESS.

"And if thy brother sin against thee, go, show him his fault between thee and him alone: if he hear thee, thou hast gained thy brother. But if he hear thee not, take with thee one or two more, that at the mouth of two witnesses or three every word may be established. And if he refuse to hear them, tell it unto the church: and if he refuse to hear the church also, let him be unto thee as the Gentile and the publican. Verily I say unto you, What things soever ye shall bind on earth shall be bound in heaven; and what things soever ye shall loose on earth shall be loosed in heaven. Again I say unto you, that if two of you shall agree on earth as touching anything that they shall ask, it shall be done for them of my Father who is in heaven. For where two or three are gathered together in my name, there am I, in the midst of them."

Then came Peter and said to him, "Lord, how oft shall my brother sin against me, and I forgive him? until seven times?"

Jesus saith unto him, "I say not unto thee, Until seven times; but, Until seventy times seven. Therefore is the kingdom of heaven likened unto a certain king, who would make a reckoning with his servants. And when he had begun to reckon, one was brought unto him, that owed him ten thousand talents. But forasmuch as he had not wherewith to pay, his lord commanded him to be sold, and his wife, and children, and all that he had, and payment to be made. The servant therefore fell down and worshipped him, saying, 'Lord, have patience with me, and I will pay thee all.' And the lord of that servant, being moved with compassion, released him, and forgave him the debt. But that servant went out, and found one of his fellow-servants, who owed him a hundred shillings: and he laid hold on him, and took him by the throat, saying, 'Pay what thou owest.' So his fellow-servant fell down and besought him, saying, 'Have patience with me, and I will pay thee.' And he would not: but went and cast him into prison, till he should pay that which was due. So when his fellow-servants saw what was done, they were exceeding sorry, and came and told unto their lord all that was done. Then his lord called him unto him, and saith to him, 'Thou wicked servant, I forgave thee all that debt, because thou besoughtest me: shouldst not thou also have had mercy on thy fellow-servant, even as I had mercy on thee?' And his lord was wroth, and delivered him to the tormentors, till he should pay all that was due. So shall also my heavenly Father do unto you, if ye forgive not every one his brother from your hearts."

THE SHEKEL FOR THE TEMPLE.

And they that received the half-shekel came to Peter, and said "Doth not your teacher pay the half-shekel?"

He saith, "Yea."

And when he came into the house, Jesus spake first to him, saying, "What thinkest thou, Simon? the kings of the earth, from whom do they receive toll or tribute? from their sons, or from strangers?"

And when he said, "From strangers," Jesus said unto him, "Therefore, the sons are free. But, lest we cause them to stumble, go thou to the sea, and cast a hook, and take up the fish that first cometh up; and when thou hast opened his mouth, thou shalt find a shekel: that take, and give unto them for me and thee."

=HIS FACE TOWARD JERUSALEM=

THE FINAL DEPARTURE FROM GALILEE
THE BEGINNING OF THE END.

Now the feast of the Jews, the feast of tabernacles, was at hand. His brethren therefore said unto him, "Depart hence, and go into Judaea, that thy disciples also may behold thy works which thou doest. For no man doeth anything in secret, and himself seeketh to be known openly. If thou doest these things, manifest thyself to the world." For even his brethren did not believe on him.

Jesus therefore saith unto them, "My time is not yet come; but your time is always ready. The world cannot hate you; but me it hateth, because I testify of it, that its works are evil. Go ye up unto the feast; I go not up yet unto this feast; because my time is not yet fulfilled." And having said these things unto them, he abode still in Galilee.

And it came to pass, when the days were well-nigh come that he should be received up, he stedfastly set his face to go to Jerusalem, and sent messengers before his face: and they went, and entered into a village of the Samaritans, to make ready for him. And they did not receive him, because his face was as though he were going to Jerusalem. And when his disciples James and John saw this, they said, "Lord, wilt thou that we bid fire to come down from heaven, and consume them?"

But he turned, and rebuked them. And they went to another village.

THE GRATEFUL SAMARITAN LEPER.

And it came to pass, as they were on the way to Jerusalem, that he was passing along the borders of Samaria and Galilee. And as he entered into a certain village, there met him ten men that were lepers, who stood afar off: and they lifted up their voices, saying, "Jesus, Master, have mercy on us."

And when he saw them, he said unto them, "Go and show yourselves unto the priests."

And it came to pass, as they went, they were cleansed. And one of them, when he saw that he was healed, turned back, with a loud voice glorifying God; and he fell upon his face at his feet, giving him thanks: and he was a Samaritan.

And Jesus answering said, "Were not the ten cleansed? but where are the nine? Were there none found that returned to give glory to God, save this stranger?"

And he said unto him, "Arise, and go thy way: thy faith hath made thee whole."

NEW DISCIPLES.

And as they went on the way, a certain scribe said unto him, "I will follow thee whithersoever thou goest."

And Jesus said unto him, "The foxes have holes, and the birds of the heaven have nests; but the Son of man hath not where to lay his head."

And he said unto another, "Follow me."

But he said, "Lord, suffer me first to go and bury my father."

But he said unto him, "Leave the dead to bury their own dead; but go thou and publish abroad the kingdom of God."

And another also said, "I will follow thee, Lord; but first suffer me to bid farewell to them that are at my house."

But Jesus said unto him, "No man, having put his hand to the plow, and looking back, is fit for the kingdom of God."

IN JERUSALEM--THE ATTEMPT TO STONE HIM JESUS AT THE FEAST OF TABERNACLES.

Then went he up unto the feast, not publicly, but as it were in secret. The Jews therefore sought him at the feast, and said, "Where is he?" And there was much murmuring among the multitudes concerning him: some said, "He is a good man;" others said, "Not so, but he leadeth the multitude astray." Yet no man spake openly of him for fear of the Jews.

But when it was now the midst of the feast Jesus went up into the temple, and taught. The Jews therefore marvelled, saying, "How knoweth this man letters, having never learned?"

Jesus therefore answered them, and said, "My teaching is not mine, but his that sent me. If any man willeth to do his will, he shall know of the teaching, whether it is of God, or whether I speak from myself. He that speaketh from himself seeketh his own glory: but he that seeketh the glory of him that sent him, the same is true, and no unrighteousness is in him. Did not Moses give you the law, and yet none of you doeth the law? Why seek ye to kill me?"

The multitude answered, "Thou hast a demon: who seeketh to kill thee?"

Jesus answered and said unto them, "I did one work, and ye all marvel because thereof. Moses hath given you circumcision (not that it is of Moses, but of the fathers); and on the sabbath ye circumcise a man. If a man receiveth circumcision on the sabbath, that the law of Moses may not be broken; are ye wroth with me, because I made a man every whit whole on the sabbath? Judge not according to appearance, but judge righteous judgment."

Some therefore of them of Jerusalem said, "Is not this he whom they seek to kill? And lo, he speaketh openly, and they say nothing unto him. Can it be that the rulers indeed know that this is the Christ? Howbeit we know this man whence he is; but when the Christ cometh, no one knoweth whence he is."

Jesus therefore cried in the temple, teaching and saying, "Ye both know me, and know whence I am; and I am not come of myself, but he that sent me is true, whom ye know not. I know him: because I am from him, and he sent me."

They sought therefore to take him: and no man laid his hand on him, because his hour was not yet come. But of the multitude many believed on him; and they said, "When the Christ shall come, will he do more signs than those which this man hath done?"

The Pharisees heard the multitude murmuring these things concerning him; and the chief priests and the Pharisees sent officers to take him.

Jesus therefore said, "Yet a little while am I with you, and I go unto him that sent me. Ye shall seek me, and shall not find me: and where I am, ye can not come."

The Jews therefore said among themselves, "Whither will this man go that we shall not find him? will he go unto the Dispersion among the Greeks, and teach the Greeks? What is this word that he said, 'Ye shall seek me, and shall not find me; and where I am, ye cannot come'?"

Now on the last day, the great day of the feast, Jesus stood and cried, saying, "If any man thirst, let him come unto me and drink. He that believeth on me, as the scripture hath said, from within him shall flow rivers of living water."

But this spake he of the Spirit, which they that believed on him were to receive: for the Spirit was not yet given; because Jesus was not yet glorified.

Some of the multitude therefore, when they heard these words, said, "This is of a truth the prophet." Others said, "This is the Christ." But some said, "What, doth the Christ come out of Galilee? Hath not the scripture said that the Christ cometh of the seed of David, and from Bethlehem, the village where David was?"

So there arose a division in the multitude because of him. And some of them would have taken him; but no man laid hands on him.

The officers therefore came to the chief priests and Pharisees; and they said unto them, "Why did ye not bring him?"

The officers answered, "Never man so spake."

The Pharisees therefore answered them, "Are ye also led astray? Hath any of the rulers believed on him, or of the Pharisees? But this multitude that knoweth not the law are accursed."

Nicodemus saith unto them (he that came to him before, being one of them), "Doth our law judge a man, except it first hear from himself and know what he doeth?"

They answered and said unto him, "Art thou also of Galilee? Search, and see that out of Galilee ariseth no prophet."

JESUS AND THE ACCUSED WOMAN.

And they went every man unto his own house: but Jesus went unto the mount of Olives.

And early in the morning he came again into the temple, and all the people came unto him; and he sat down, and taught them. And the scribes and the Pharisees bring a woman taken in adultery; and having set her in the midst, they say unto him, "Teacher, this woman hath been taken in adultery, in the very act. Now in the law Moses commanded us to stone such: what then sayest thou of her?" And this they said, trying him, that they might have whereof to accuse him.

But Jesus stooped down, and with his finger wrote on the ground. But when they continued asking him, he lifted up himself and said unto them, "He that is without sin among you, let him first cast a stone at her."

And again he stooped down, and with his finger wrote on the ground. And they, when they heard it, went out one by one, beginning from the eldest, even unto the last: and Jesus was left alone, and the woman, where she was, in the midst. And Jesus lifted up himself, and said unto her, "Woman, where are they? did no man condemn thee?"

And she said, "No man, Lord."

And Jesus said, "Neither do I condemn thee: go thy way; from henceforth sin no more."

THE LIGHT OF THE WORLD.

Again therefore Jesus spake unto them, saying, "I am the light of the world: he that followeth me shall not walk in the darkness, but shall have the light of life."

The Pharisees therefore said unto him, "Thou bearest witness of thyself; thy witness is not true."

Jesus answered and said unto them, "Even if I bear witness of myself, my witness is true; for I know whence I came, and whither I go; but ye know not whence I come, or whither I go. Ye judge after the flesh; I judge no man. Yea and if I judge, my judgment is true; for I am not alone, but I and the Father that sent me. Yea and in your law it is written, that the witness of two men is true. I am he that beareth witness of myself, and the Father that sent me beareth witness of me."

They said therefore unto him, "Where is thy Father?"

Jesus answered, "Ye know neither me, nor my Father: if ye knew me, ye would know my Father also."

These words spake he in the treasury, as he taught in the temple: and no man took him; because his hour was not yet come.

He said therefore again unto them, "I go away, and ye shall seek me, and shall die in your sin: whither I go, ye cannot come."

The Jews therefore said, "Will he kill himself, that he saith, 'Whither I go, ye cannot come?'"

And he said unto them, "Ye are from beneath; I am from above: ye are of this world; I am not of this world. I said therefore unto you, that ye shall die in your sins: for except ye believe that I am he, ye shall die in your sins."

They said therefore unto him, "Who art thou?"

Jesus said unto them, "Even that which I have also spoken unto you from the beginning I have many things to speak and to judge concerning you; howbeit he that sent me is true; and the things which I heard from him, these speak I unto the world."

They perceived not that he spake to them of the Father.

Jesus therefore said, "When ye have lifted up the Son of man, then shall ye know that I am he, and that I do nothing of myself, but as the Father taught me, I speak these things. And he that sent me is with me; he hath not left me alone; for I do always the things that are pleasing to him."

As he spake these things, many believed on him.

THE FREEDOM OF THE SOUL.

Jesus therefore said to those Jews that had believed him, "If ye abide in my word, then are ye truly my disciples; and ye shall know the truth, and the truth shall make you free."

They answered unto him, "We are Abraham's seed, and have never yet been in bondage to any man; how sayest thou, 'Ye shall be made free'?"

Jesus answered them, "Verily, verily, I say unto you, Every one that committeth sin is the bondservant of sin. And the bondservant abideth not in the house for ever: the son abideth for ever. If therefore the Son shall make you free, ye shall be free indeed. I know that ye are Abraham's seed; yet ye seek to kill me, because my word hath not free course in you. I speak the things which I have seen with my Father: and ye also do the things which ye heard from your father."

They answered and said unto him, "Our father is Abraham."

Jesus saith unto them, "If ye were Abraham's children, ye would do the works of Abraham. But now ye seek to kill me, a man that hath told you the truth, which I heard from God: this did not Abraham. Ye do the works of your father."

They said unto him, "We were not born of fornication; we have one Father, even God."

Jesus said unto them, "If God were your Father, ye would love me: for I came forth and am come from God; for neither have I come of myself, but he sent me. Why do ye not understand my speech? Even because ye cannot hear my word. Ye are of your father the devil, and the lusts of your father it is your will to do. He was a murderer from the beginning, and standeth not in the truth, because there is no truth in him. When he speaketh a lie, he speaketh of his own: for he is a liar, and the father thereof. But because I say the truth, ye believe me not. Which of you convicteth me of sin? If I say truth, why do ye not believe me? He that is of God heareth the words of God: for this cause ye hear them not, because ye are not of God."

The Jews answered and said unto him, "Say we not well that thou art a Samaritan, and hast a demon?"

Jesus answered, "I have not a demon: but I honor my Father, and ye dishonor me. But I seek not mine own glory: there is one that seeketh and judgeth. Verily, verily, I say unto you, If a man keep my word, he shall never see death."

The Jews said unto him, "Now we know that thou hast a demon. Abraham died, and the prophets; and thou sayest, 'If a man keep my word, he shall never taste of death.' Art thou greater than our father Abraham, who died? and the prophets died: whom makest thou thyself?"

Jesus answered, "If I glorify myself, my glory is nothing: it is my Father that glorifieth me; of whom ye say, that he is your God; and ye have not known him: but I know him; and if I should say, 'I know him not,' I shall be like unto you, a liar; but I know him, and keep his word. Your father Abraham rejoiced to see my day; and he saw it, and was glad."

The Jews therefore said unto him, "Thou art not yet fifty years old, and hast thou seen Abraham?"

Jesus said unto them, "Verily, verily, I say unto you. Before Abraham was born, I am."

They took up stones therefore to cast at him; but Jesus hid himself, and went out of the temple.

THE MINISTRY IN PEREA
THE MISSION OF THE SEVENTY.

And he arose and cometh into the borders of Judaea and beyond the Jordan; and great multitudes followed him; and he healed them there.

And the Lord appointed seventy others, and sent them two and two before his face into every city and place, whither he himself was about to come. And he said unto them, "The harvest indeed is plenteous, but the laborers are few; pray ye therefore the Lord of the harvest, that he send forth laborers into his harvest. Go your ways; behold, I send you forth as lambs into the midst of wolves. Carry no purse, no wallet, no shoes; and salute no man on the way. And into whatsoever house ye shall enter, first say, 'Peace be to this house.' And if a son of peace be there, your peace shall rest upon him; but if not, it shall turn to you again. And in that same house remain, eating and drinking such things as they give: for the laborer is worthy of his hire. Go not from house to house. And into whatsoever city ye enter, and they receive you, eat such things as are set before you: and heal the sick that are therein, and say unto them, 'The kingdom of God is come nigh unto you.' But into whatsoever city ye shall enter, and they receive you not, go out into the streets thereof and say, 'Even the dust from your city, that cleaveth to our feet, we wipe off against you: nevertheless know this, that the kingdom of God is come nigh.' I say unto you, It shall be more tolerable in that day for Sodom, than for that city. He that heareth you heareth me; and he that rejecteth you rejecteth me; and he that rejecteth me rejecteth him that sent me."

THE RETURN OF THE SEVENTY.

And the seventy returned with joy, saying, "Lord, even the demons are subject unto us in thy name."

And he said unto them, "I beheld Satan fallen as lightning from heaven. Behold, I have given you authority to tread upon serpents and scorpions, and over all the power of the enemy: and nothing shall in any wise hurt you. Nevertheless in this rejoice not, that the spirits are subject unto you: but rejoice that your names are written in heaven."

THE MEEK AND LOWLY.

In that same hour he rejoiced in the Holy Spirit, and said, "I thank thee, O Father, Lord of heaven and earth, that thou didst hide these things from the wise and understanding, and didst reveal them unto babes; yea, Father; for so it was well-pleasing in thy sight. All things have been delivered unto me of my Father: and no one knoweth who the Son is, save the Father; and who the Father is, save the Son, and he to whomsoever the Son willeth to reveal him."

And turning to the disciples, he said privately, "Blessed are the eyes which see the things that ye see: for I say unto you, that many prophets and kings desired to see the things which ye see, and saw them not; and to hear the things which ye hear, and heard them not.

"Come unto me, all ye that labor and are heavy laden, and I will give you rest. Take my yoke upon you, and learn of me; for I am meek and lowly in heart: and ye shall find rest unto your souls. For my yoke is easy, and my burden is light."

THE UNREPENTANT CITIES.

Then began he to upbraid the cities wherein most of his mighty works were done, because they repented not. "Woe unto thee, Chorazin! woe unto thee, Bethsaida! for if the mighty works had been done in Tyre and Sidon which were done in you, they would have repented long ago in sackcloth and ashes. But I say unto you, it shall be more tolerable for Tyre and Sidon in the day of judgment, than for you. And thou, Capernaum, shalt thou be exalted unto heaven? thou shalt go down unto Hades: for if the mighty works had been done in Sodom which were done in thee, it would have remained until this day. But I say unto you that it shall be more tolerable for the land of Sodom in the day of judgment, than for thee."

THE GOOD SAMARITAN.

And behold, a certain lawyer stood up and made trial of him, saying, "Teacher, what shall I do to inherit eternal life?"

And he said unto him, "What is written in the law? how readest thou?"

And he answering said, "Thou shalt love the Lord thy God with all thy heart, and with all thy soul, and with all thy strength, and with all thy mind; and thy neighbor as thyself."

And he said unto him, "Thou hast answered right: this do and thou shalt live."

But he, desiring to justify himself, said unto Jesus, "And who is my neighbor?"

Jesus made answer and said, "A certain man was going down from Jerusalem to Jericho; and he fell among robbers, who both stripped him and beat him, and departed, leaving him half dead. And by chance a certain priest was going down that way: and when he saw him, he passed by on the other side. And in like manner a

Levite also, when he came to the place, and saw him, passed by on the other side. But a certain Samaritan, as he journeyed, came where he was: and when he saw him, he was moved with compassion, and came to him, and bound up his wounds, pouring on them oil and wine; and he set him on his own beast, and brought him to an inn, and took care of him. And on the morrow he took out two shillings, and gave them to the host, and said, 'Take care of him: and whatsoever thou spendest more, I, when I come back again, will repay thee.' Which of these three, thinkest thou, proved neighbor unto him that fell among the robbers?"

And he said, "He that showed mercy on him."

And Jesus said unto him, "Go, and do thou likewise."

IN JERUSALEM--THE ATTEMPT TO ARREST HIM. THE FRIENDS AT BETHANY.

Now as they went on their way, he entered into a certain village: and a certain woman named Martha received him into her house.

And she had a sister called Mary, who also sat at the Lord's feet and heard his word.

But Martha was cumbered about much serving; and she came up to him, and said, "Lord, dost thou not care that my sister did leave me to serve alone? bid her therefore that she help me."

But the Lord answered and said unto her, "Martha, Martha, thou art anxious and troubled about many things: but one thing is needful: for Mary hath chosen the good part, which shall not be taken away from her."

A MIRACLE IN JERUSALEM.

And as he passed by, he saw a man blind from his birth. And his disciples asked him, saying, "Rabbi, who sinned, this man, or his parents, that he should be born blind?"

Jesus answered, "Neither did this man sin, nor his parents: but that the works of God should be made manifest in him. We must work the works of him that sent me, while it is day: the night cometh, when no man can work. When I am in the world, I am the light of the world."

When he had thus spoken he spat on the ground, and made clay of the spittle, and anointed his eyes with the clay, and said unto him, "Go, wash in the pool of Siloam" (which is by interpretation, Sent).

He went away therefore, and washed, and came seeing.

The neighbors therefore, and they that saw him aforetime, that he was a beggar, said, "Is not this he that sat and begged?"

Others said, "It is he:" others said, "No, but he is like him."

He said, "I am he."

They said therefore unto him, "How then were thine eyes opened?"

He answered, "The man that is called Jesus made clay and anointed mine eyes, and said unto me, 'Go to Siloam, and wash:' so I went away and washed, and I received sight."

And they said unto him, "Where is he?"

He saith, "I know not."

They bring to the Pharisees him that aforetime was blind. Now it was the sabbath on the day when Jesus made the clay, and opened his eyes. Again therefore the Pharisees also asked him how he received his sight.

And he said unto them, "He put clay upon mine eyes, and I washed, and I see."

Some therefore of the Pharisees said. "This man is not from God, because he keepeth not the sabbath."

But others said, "How can a man that is a sinner do such signs?"

And there was a division among them.

They say therefore unto the blind man again, "What sayest thou of him, in that he opened thine eyes?"

And he said, "He is a prophet."

The Jews therefore did not believe concerning him, that he had been blind, and had received his sight, until they called the parents of him that had received his sight, and asked them, saying, "Is this your son, who ye say was born blind? how then doth he now see?"

His parents answered and said, "We know that this is our son, and that he was born blind: but how he now seeth, we know not; or who opened his eyes, we know not: ask him; he is of age; he shall speak for himself."

These things said his parents, because they feared the Jews; for the Jews had agreed already, that if any man should confess him to be Christ, he should be put out of the synagogue. Therefore said his parents, "He is of age; ask him."

So they called a second time the man that was blind, and said unto him, "Give glory to God: we know that this man is a sinner."

He therefore answered, "Whether he is a sinner, I know not: one thing I know, that, whereas I was blind, now I see."

They said therefore unto him, "What did he to thee? how opened he thine eyes."

He answered them, "I told you even now, and ye did not hear; wherefore would ye hear it again? would ye also become his disciples?"

And they reviled him, and said, "Thou art his disciple; but we are disciples of Moses. We know that God hath spoken unto Moses: but as for this man, we know not whence he is."

The man answered and said unto them. "Why, herein is the marvel, that ye know not whence he is, and yet he opened mine eyes. We know that God heareth not sinners: but if any man be a worshipper of God, and do his will, him he heareth. Since the world began it was never heard that any one opened the eyes of a man born blind. If this man were not from God, he could do nothing."

They answered and said unto him, "Thou wast altogether born in sins, and dost thou teach us?" And they cast him out.

Jesus heard that they had cast him out: and finding him, he said, "Dost thou believe on the Son of God?"

He answered and said, "And who is he, Lord, that I may believe on him?"

Jesus said unto him, "Thou hast both seen him, and he it is that speaketh with thee."

And he said, "Lord, I believe."

And he worshipped him.

And Jesus said, "For judgment came I into this world, that they that see not may see; and that they that see may become blind."

Those of the Pharisees who were with him heard these things, and said unto him, "Are we also blind?"

Jesus said unto them, "If ye were blind, ye would have no sin: but now ye say, 'We see:' your sin remaineth."

THE GOOD SHEPHERD.

"Verily, verily, I say unto you, He that entereth not by the door into the fold of the sheep, but climbeth up some other way, the same is a thief and a robber. But he that entereth in by the door is the shepherd of the sheep. To him the porter openeth; and the sheep hear his voice: and he calleth his own sheep by name, and leadeth them out. When he hath put forth all his own, he goeth before them, and the sheep follow him: for they know his voice. And a stranger will they not follow, but will flee from him: for they know not the voice of strangers."

This parable spake Jesus unto them: but they understood not what things they were which he spake unto them.

Jesus therefore said unto them again, "Verily, verily, I say unto you, I am the door of the sheep. All that came before me are thieves and robbers: but the sheep did not hear them. I am the door; by me if any man enter in, he shall be saved, and shall go in and go out, and shall find pasture. The thief cometh not, but that he may steal, and kill, and destroy: I came that they may have life, and may have it abundantly. I am the good shepherd: the good shepherd layeth down his life for the sheep. He that is a hireling, and not a shepherd, whose own the sheep are not, beholdeth the wolf coming, and leaveth the sheep, and fleeth, and the wolf snatcheth them, and scattereth them; he fleeth because he is a hireling, and careth not for the sheep. I am the good shepherd; and I know mine own, and mine own know me, even as the Father knoweth me, and I know the Father; and I lay down my life for the sheep. And other sheep I have, which are not of this fold: them also I must bring, and they shall hear my voice: and they shall become one flock, one shepherd. Therefore doth the Father love me, because I lay down my life, that I may take it again. No one taketh it away from me, but I lay it down of myself. I have power to lay it down, and I have power to take it again. This commandment received I from my Father."

There arose a division again among the Jews because of these words. And many of them said, "He hath a demon, and is mad; why hear ye him?"

Others said, "These are not the sayings of one possessed with a demon. Can a demon open the eyes of the blind?"

JESUS AT THE FEAST OF DEDICATION.

And it was the feast of the dedication at Jerusalem; it was winter; and Jesus was walking in the temple, in Solomon's porch. The Jews therefore came round about him, and said unto him, "How long dost thou hold us in suspense? If thou art the Christ, tell us plainly."

Jesus answered them, "I told you, and ye believe not; the works that I do in my Father's name, these bear witness of me. But ye believe not, because ye are not of my sheep. My sheep hear my voice, and I know them, and they follow me: and I give unto them eternal life; and they shall never perish, and no one shall snatch them out of my hand. My Father, who hath given them unto me, is greater than all; and no one is able to snatch them out of the Father's hand. I and the Father are one."

The Jews took up stones again to stone him.

Jesus answered them, "Many good works have I showed you from the Father; for which of those works do ye stone me?"

The Jews answered him, "For a good work we stone thee not, but for blasphemy; and because that thou, being a man, makest thyself God."

Jesus answered them, "Is it not written in your law, 'I said, Ye are gods?' If he called them gods, unto whom the word of God came (and the scripture cannot be broken), say ye of him, whom the Father sanctified and sent into the world, 'Thou blasphemest;' because I said, 'I am the Son of God?' If I do not the works of my Father, believe me not. But if I do them, though ye believe not me, believe the works: that ye may know and understand that the Father is in me, and I in the Father."

They sought again to take him: and he went forth out of their hand.

RENEWED MINISTRY IN PEREA

JESUS AND THE PHARISEES.

And he went away again beyond the Jordan into the place where John was at the first baptizing; and there he abode. And many came unto him; and they said, "John indeed did no sign: but all things whatsoever John spake of this man were true." And many believed on him there.

Now a Pharisee asketh him to dine with him: and he went in, and sat down to meat. And when the Pharisee saw it, he marvelled that he had not first bathed himself before dinner.

And the Lord said unto him, "Now ye the Pharisees cleanse the outside of the cup and of the platter; but your inward part is full of extortion and wickedness. Ye foolish ones, did not he that made the outside make the inside also? But give for alms those things which are within; and behold, all things are clean unto you."

And when he was come out from thence, the scribes and the Pharisees began to press upon him vehemently, and to provoke him to speak of many things; laying wait for him, to catch something out of his mouth.

In the meantime, when the many thousands of the multitude were gathered together, insomuch that they trod one upon another, he began to say unto his disciples first of all, "Beware ye of the leaven of the Pharisees, which is hypocrisy. But there is nothing covered up, that shall not be revealed; and hid, that shall not be known."

WARNING AGAINST COVETOUSNESS.

And one out of the multitude said unto him, "Teacher, bid my brother divide the inheritance with me."

But he said unto him, "Man, who made me a judge or a divider over you?"

And he said unto them, "Take heed and keep yourselves from all covetousness: for a man's life consisteth not in the abundance of the things which he possesseth."

And he spake a parable unto them, saying, "The ground of a certain rich man brought forth plentifully; and he reasoned within himself, saying, 'What shall I do, because I have not where to bestow my fruits?' And he said, 'This will I do: I will pull down my barns, and build greater; and there will I bestow all my grain and my goods. And I will say to my soul, "Soul, thou hast much goods laid up for many years; take thine ease, eat, drink, be merry."' But God said unto him, 'Thou foolish one, this night is thy soul required of thee: and the things which thou hast prepared, whose shall they be?' So is he that layeth up treasure for himself, and is not rich toward God."

THE FALL OF THE TOWER.

Now there were some present at that very season who told him of the Galilaeans, whose blood Pilate had mingled with their sacrifices. And he answered and said unto them, "Think ye that these Galilaeans were sinners above all the Galilaeans, because they have suffered these things? I tell you, Nay: but, except ye repent, ye shall all in like manner perish. Or those eighteen, upon whom the tower in Siloam fell, and killed them, think ye that they were offenders above all the men that dwell in Jerusalem? I tell you, Nay: but, except ye repent, ye shall all likewise perish."

And he spake this parable: "A certain man had a fig tree planted in his vineyard; and he came seeking fruit thereon, and found none. And he said unto the vinedresser, 'Behold, these three years I come seeking fruit on this fig tree, and find none: cut it down; why doth it also cumber the ground.' And he answering saith unto him, 'Lord, let it alone this year also, till I shall dig about it, and dung it: and if it bear fruit thenceforth, well; but if not, thou shalt cut it down.'"

THE USES OF THE SABBATH.

And he was teaching in one of the synagogues on the sabbath day. And behold, a woman that had a spirit of infirmity eighteen years; and she was bowed together, and could in no wise lift herself up. And when Jesus saw her, he called her, and said to her, "Woman, thou art loosed from thine infirmity."

And he laid his hands upon her: and immediately she was made straight, and glorified God.

And the ruler of the synagogue, being moved with indignation because Jesus had healed on the sabbath, answered and said to the multitude, "There are six days in which men ought to work: in them therefore come and be healed, and not on the day of the sabbath."

But the Lord answered him and said, "Ye hypocrites, doth not each one of you on the sabbath loose his ox or his ass from the stall, and lead him away to watering? And ought not this woman, being a daughter of Abraham, whom Satan had bound, lo, these eighteen years, to have been loosed from this bond on the day of the sabbath?"

And as he said these things, all his adversaries were put to shame: and all the multitude rejoiced for all the glorious things that were done by him.

A QUESTION OF SALVATION.

And he went on his way through cities and villages, teaching, and journeying on unto Jerusalem. And one said unto him, "Lord, are they few that are saved?"

And he said unto them, "Strive to enter in by the narrow door: for many, I say unto you, shall seek to enter in, and shall not be able. When once the master of the house is risen up, and hath shut to the door, and ye begin to stand without and to knock at the door, saying, 'Lord, open to us,' and he shall answer and say to you, 'I know you not whence ye are'; then shall ye begin to say, 'We did eat and drink in thy presence, and thou didst teach in our streets'; and he shall say, 'I tell you, I know not whence ye are; depart from me, all ye workers of iniquity.' There shall be the weeping and the gnashing of teeth, when ye shall see Abraham, and Isaac, and Jacob, and all the prophets, in the kingdom of God, and yourselves cast forth without. And they shall come from the east and west, and from the north and south, and shall sit down in the kingdom of God. And behold, there are last who shall be first, and there are first who shall be last."

A MESSAGE TO HEROD.

In that very hour there came certain Pharisees, saying to him, "Get thee out, and go hence: for Herod would fain kill thee."

And he said unto them, "Go and say to that fox, 'Behold, I cast out demons and perform cures to-day and to-morrow, and the third day I am perfected.' Nevertheless I must go on my way to-day and to-morrow and the day following: for it cannot be that a prophet perish out of Jerusalem."

THE OX IN THE PIT.

And it came to pass, when he went into the house of one of the rulers of the Pharisees on a sabbath to eat bread, that they were watching him. And behold, there was before him a certain man that had the dropsy. And Jesus answering spake unto the lawyers and Pharisees, saying, "Is it lawful to heal on the sabbath, or not?"

But they held their peace. And he took him, and healed him, and let him go.

And he said unto them, "Which of you shall have an ass or an ox fallen into a well, and will not straightway draw him up on a sabbath day?" And they could not answer again unto these things.

THE CHIEF PLACES AT THE FEAST.

And he spake a parable unto those that were bidden, when he marked how they chose out the chief seats; saying unto them, "When thou art bidden of any man to a marriage feast, sit not down in the chief seat; lest haply a more honorable man than thou be bidden of him, and he that bade thee and him shall come and say to thee, 'Give this man place'; and then thou shalt begin with shame to take the lowest place. But when thou art bidden, go and sit down in the lowest place; that when he that hath bidden thee cometh, he may say to thee, 'Friend, go up higher'; then shalt thou have glory in the presence of all that sit at meat with thee. For every one that exalteth himself shall be humbled: and he that humbleth himself shall be exalted."

And he said to him also that had bidden him, "When thou makest a dinner or a supper, call not thy friends, nor thy brethren, nor thy kinsmen, nor rich neighbors; lest haply they also bid thee again, and a recompense be made thee. But when thou makest a feast, bid the poor, the maimed, the lame, the blind: and thou shalt be blessed; because they have not wherewith to recompense thee: for thou shalt be recompensed in the resurrection of the just.

THE SLIGHTED INVITATION.

And when one of them that sat at meat with him heard these things, he said unto him, "Blessed is he that shall eat bread in the kingdom of God."

But he said unto him, "A certain man made a great supper; and he bade many: and he sent forth his servant at supper time to say to them that were bidden, 'Come; for all things are now ready.' And they all with one consent began to make excuse. The first said unto him, 'I have bought a field, and I must needs go out and see it; I pray thee have me excused.' And another said, 'I have bought five yoke of oxen, and I go to prove them; I pray thee have me excused.' And another said, 'I have married a wife, and therefore I cannot come.' And the servant came, and told his lord these things. Then the master of the house, being angry, said to his servant, 'Go out quickly into the streets and lanes of the city, and bring in hither the poor and maimed and blind and lame.' And the servant said, 'Lord, what thou didst command is done, and yet there is room.' And the lord said unto the servant, 'Go out into the highways and hedges, and constrain them to come in, that my house may be filled. For I say unto you, that none of those men that were bidden shall taste of my supper.'"

COUNTING THE COST.

Now there went with him great multitudes: and he turned, and said unto them, "If any man cometh unto me, and hateth not his own father, and mother, and wife, and children, and brethren, and sisters, yea, and his own life also, he cannot be my disciple. Whosoever doth not bear his own cross, and come after me, cannot be my disciple. For which of you, desiring to build a tower, doth not first sit down and count the cost, whether he have wherewith to complete it? Lest haply, when he hath laid a foundation, and is not able to finish, all that behold begin to mock him, saying, 'This man began to build, and was not able to finish.' Or what king, as he goeth to encounter another king in war, will not sit down first and take counsel whether he is able with ten thousand to meet him that cometh against him with twenty thousand? Or else, while the other is yet a great way off, he sendeth an ambassage, and asketh conditions of peace. So therefore whosoever he be of you that renounceth not all that he hath, he cannot be my disciple. Salt therefore is good: but if even the salt have lost its savor, wherewith shall it be seasoned? It is fit neither for the land nor for the dunghill: men cast it out. He that hath ears to hear, let him hear."

THE NINETY AND NINE.

Now all the publicans and sinners were drawing near unto him to hear him. And both the Pharisees and the scribes murmured, saying, "This man receiveth sinners, and eateth with them."

And he spake unto them this parable, saying, "What man of you, having a hundred sheep, and having lost one of them, doth not leave the ninety and nine in the wilderness, and go after that which is lost, until he find it? And when he hath found it, he layeth it on his shoulders, rejoicing. And when he cometh home, he calleth together his friends and his neighbors, saying unto them, 'Rejoice with me, for I have found my sheep which was lost.' I say unto you, that even so there shall be joy in heaven over one sinner that repenteth, more than over ninety and nine righteous persons, who need no repentance.

THE LOST COIN.

"Or what woman having ten pieces of silver, if she lose one piece, doth not light a lamp, and sweep the house, and seek diligently until she find it? And when she hath found it, she calleth together her friends and neighbors, saying, 'Rejoice with me, for I have found the piece which I had lost.' Even so, I say unto you, there is joy in the presence of the angels of God over one sinner that repenteth."

THE PRODIGAL SON.

And he said, "A certain man had two sons: and the younger of them said to his father, 'Father, give me the portion of thy substance that falleth to me.' And he divided unto them his living. And not many days after, the younger son gathered all together and took his journey into a far country; and there he wasted his substance with riotous living. And when he had spent all, there arose a mighty famine in that country; and he began to be in want. And he went and joined himself to one of the citizens of that country; and he sent him into his fields to feed swine. And he would fain have filled his belly with the husks that the swine did eat: and no man gave unto him. But when he came to himself he said, 'How many hired servants of my father's have bread enough and to spare, and I perish here with hunger! I will arise and go to my father, and will say unto him, Father, I have sinned against heaven, and in thy sight: I am no more worthy to be called thy son: make me as one of thy hired servants.' And he arose, and came to his father. But while he was yet afar off, his father saw him, and was moved with compassion, and ran, and fell on his neck, and kissed him. And the son said unto him, 'Father, I have sinned against heaven, and in thy sight: I am no more worthy to be called thy son.' But the father said to his servants, 'Bring forth quickly the best robe, and put it on him; and put a ring on his hand, and shoes on his feet: and bring the fatted calf, and kill it, and let us eat, and make merry: for this my son was dead, and is alive again; he was lost, and is found.' And they began to be merry. Now his elder son was in the field: and as he came and drew nigh to the house, he heard music and dancing. And he called to him one of the servants, and inquired what these things might be. And he said unto him, 'Thy brother is come; and thy father hath killed the fatted calf, because he hath received him safe and sound.' But he was angry, and would not go in: and his father came out, and entreated him. But he answered and said to his father, 'Lo, these many years do I serve thee, and I never transgressed a commandment of thine; and yet thou never gavest me a kid, that I might make merry with my friends; but when this thy son came, who hath devoured thy living with harlots, thou killedst for him the fatted calf.' And he said unto him, 'Son, thou art ever with me, and all that is mine is thine. But it was meet to make merry and be glad: for this thy brother was dead, and is alive again; and was lost, and is found.'"

THE UNJUST STEWARD.

And he said also unto the disciples, "There was a certain rich man, who had a steward; and the same was accused unto him that he was wasting his goods. And he called him, and said unto him, 'What is this that I hear of thee? render the account of thy stewardship; for thou canst be no longer steward' And the steward said within himself, 'What shall I do, seeing that my lord taketh away the stewardship from me? I have not strength to dig; to beg I am ashamed. I am resolved what to do, that, when I am put out of the stewardship, they may receive me into their houses.' And calling to him each one of his lord's debtors, he said to the first, 'How much owest thou unto my lord?' And he said, 'A hundred measures of oil.' And he said unto him, 'Take thy bond, and sit down quickly and write fifty.' Then said he to another, 'And how much owest thou?' And he said, 'A hundred measures of wheat.' He saith unto him, 'Take thy bond, and write fourscore.' And his lord commended the unrighteous steward because he had done wisely: for the sons of this world are for their own generation wiser than the sons of the light. And I say unto you, Make to yourselves friends by means of the mammon of unrighteousness; that, when it shall fail, they may receive you into the eternal tabernacles. He that is faithful in a very little is faithful also in much: and he that is unrighteous in a very little is unrighteous also in much. If therefore ye have not been faithful in the unrighteous mammon, who will commit to your trust the true riches? And if ye have not been faithful in that which is another's, who will give you that which is your own? No servant can serve two masters: for either he will hate the one, and love the other; or else he will hold to one, and despise the other. Ye cannot serve God and mammon."

A PARABLE TO THE LOVERS OF MONEY.

And the Pharisees, who were lovers of money, heard all these things; and they scoffed at him.

And he said unto them, "Ye are they that justify yourselves in the sight of men; but God knoweth your hearts: for that which is exalted among men is an abomination in the sight of God.

"Now there was a certain rich man, and he was clothed in purple and fine linen, faring sumptuously every day: and a certain beggar named Lazarus was laid at his gate, full of sores, and desiring to be fed with the crumbs that fell from the rich man's table; yea, even the dogs came and licked his sores. And it came to pass, that the beggar died, and that he was carried away by the angels into Abraham's bosom: and the rich man also died, and was buried. And in Hades he lifted up his eyes, being in torments, and seeth Abraham afar off, and Lazarus in his bosom. And he cried and said, 'Father Abraham, have mercy on me, and send Lazarus, that he may dip the tip of his finger in water, and cool my tongue; for I am in anguish in this flame.' But Abraham said, 'Son, remember that thou in thy lifetime receivedst thy good things, and Lazarus in like manner evil things; but now he is comforted, and thou art in anguish. And besides all this, between us and you there is a great gulf fixed, that they that would pass from hence to you may not be able, and that none may cross over from thence to us.' And he said, 'I pray thee therefore, father, that thou wouldest send him to my father's house; for I have five brethren; that he may testify unto them, lest they also come into this place of torment.' But Abraham saith, 'They have Moses and the prophets; let them hear them.' And he said, 'Nay, father Abraham: but if one go to them from the dead, they will repent.' And he said unto him, 'If they hear not Moses and the prophets, neither will they be persuaded, if one rise from the dead.'"

"INCREASE OUR FAITH."

And the apostles said unto the Lord, "Increase our faith."

And the Lord said. "If ye had faith as a grain of mustard seed, ye would say unto this sycamine tree, 'Be thou rooted up, and be thou planted in the sea'; and it would obey you. But who is there of you, having a servant plowing or keeping sheep, that will say unto him, when he is come in from the field. 'Come straightway and sit down to meat'; and will not rather say unto him, 'Make ready wherewith I may sup, and gird thyself, and serve me, till I have eaten and drunken; and afterward thou shalt eat and drink?' Doth he thank the servant because he did the things that were commanded? Even so ye also, when ye shall have done all the things that are commanded you, say, 'We are unprofitable servants; we have done that which it was our duty to do.'"

NEAR JERUSALEM--THE PLOT TO KILL HIM. THE RAISING OF LAZARUS.

Now a certain man was sick, Lazarus of Bethany, of the village of Mary and her sister Martha. And it was that Mary who anointed the Lord with ointment, and wiped his feet with her hair, whose brother Lazarus was sick.

The sisters therefore sent unto him, saying, "Lord, behold, he whom thou lovest is sick."

But when Jesus heard it, he said, "This sickness is not unto death, but for the glory of God, that the son of God may be glorified thereby."

Now Jesus loved Martha, and her sister, and Lazarus. When therefore he heard that he was sick, he abode at that time two days in the place where he was.

Then after this he saith to the disciples, "Let us go into Judaea again."

The disciples say unto him, "Rabbi, the Jews were but now seeking to stone thee: and goest thou thither again?"

Jesus answered, "Are there not twelve hours in the day? If a man walk in the day, he stumbleth not, because he seeth the light of this world. But if a man walk in the night, he stumbleth, because the light is not in him."

These things spake he: and after this he saith unto them. "Our friend Lazarus is fallen asleep; but I go, that I may awake him out of sleep."

The disciples therefore said unto him, "Lord, if he is fallen asleep, he will recover."

Now Jesus had spoken of his death: but they thought that he spake of taking rest in sleep.

Then Jesus therefore said unto them plainly, "Lazarus is dead. And I am glad for your sakes that I was not there, to the intent ye may believe; nevertheless let us go unto him."

Thomas therefore, who is called Didymus, said unto his fellow-disciples, "Let us also go, that we may die with him."

So when Jesus came, he found that he had been in the tomb four days already.

Now Bethany was nigh unto Jerusalem, about fifteen furlongs off; and many of the Jews had come to Martha and Mary, to console them concerning their brother.

Martha therefore, when she heard that Jesus was coming, went and met him: but Mary still sat in the house. Martha therefore said unto Jesus, "Lord, if thou hadst been here, my brother had not died. And even now I know that, whatsoever thou shalt ask of God, God will give thee."

Jesus saith unto her, "Thy brother shall rise again."

Martha saith unto him, "I know that he shall rise again in the resurrection at the last day."

Jesus said unto her, "I am the resurrection, and the life: he that believeth on me, though he die, yet shall he live; and whosoever liveth and believeth on me shall never die. Believest thou this?"

She saith unto him, "Yea, Lord. I have believed that thou art the Christ, the Son of God, even he that cometh into the world."

And when she had said this, she went away, and called Mary her sister secretly, saying, "The Teacher is here, and calleth thee."

And she, when she heard it, arose quickly, and went unto him. (Now Jesus was not yet come into the village, but was still in the place where Martha met him.) The Jews then who were with her in the house, and were consoling her, when they saw Mary, that she rose up quickly and went out, followed her, supposing that she was going unto the tomb to weep there.

Mary therefore, when she came where Jesus was, and saw him, fell down at his feet, saying unto him. "Lord, if thou hadst been here, my brother had not died."

When Jesus therefore saw her weeping, and the Jews also weeping who came with her, he groaned in the spirit, and was troubled, and said, "Where have ye laid him?"

They say unto him, "Lord, come and see."

Jesus wept.

The Jews therefore said, "Behold how he loved him!" But some of them said, "Could not this man, who has opened the eyes of him that was blind, have caused that this man also should not die?"

Jesus therefore again groaning in himself cometh to the tomb. Now it was a cave, and a stone lay against it. Jesus saith, "Take ye away the stone."

Martha, the sister of him that was dead, saith unto him, "Lord, by this time the body decayeth; for he hath been dead four days."

Jesus saith unto her, "Said I not unto thee, that, if thou believedst, thou shouldest see the glory of God?"

So they took away the stone. And Jesus lifted up his eyes, and said, "Father, I thank thee that thou heardest me. And I knew that thou hearest me always: but because of the multitude that standeth around I said it, that they may believe that thou didst send me."

And when he had thus spoken, he cried with a loud voice, "Lazarus, come forth."

He that was dead came forth, bound hand and foot with grave-clothes; and his face was bound about with a napkin. Jesus saith unto them, "Loose him, and let him go."

Many therefore of the Jews, who came to Mary and beheld that which he did, believed on him. But some of them went away to the Pharisees, and told them the things which Jesus had done.

THE DECISION OF THE COUNCIL.

The chief priests therefore and the Pharisees gathered a council, and said, "What do we? for this man doeth many signs. If we let him thus alone, all men will believe on him: and the Romans will come and take away both our place and our nation."

But a certain one of them, Caiaphas, being high priest that year, said unto them, "Ye know nothing at all, nor do ye take account that it is expedient for you that one man should die for the people, and that the whole nation perish not."

Now this he said not of himself: but being high priest that year, he prophesied that Jesus should die for the nation; and not for the nation only, but that he might also gather together into one the children of God that are scattered abroad.

So from that day forth they took counsel that they might put him to death.

HIS WITHDRAWAL TO EPHRAIM
THE COMING OF THE KINGDOM.

Jesus therefore walked no more openly among the Jews, but departed thence into the country near to the wilderness, into a city called Ephraim; and there he tarried with the disciples.

And being asked by the Pharisees, when the kingdom of God cometh, he answered them and said, "The kingdom of God cometh not with observation: neither shall they say, 'Lo, here!' or, 'There!' for lo, the kingdom of God is within you."

And he said unto the disciples, "The days will come, when ye shall desire to see one of the days of the Son of man, and ye shall not see it. And they shall say to you, 'Lo, there!' 'Lo, here!' go not away, nor follow after them; for as the lightning, when it lighteneth out of the one part under the heaven, shineth unto the other part under heaven; so shall the Son of man be in his day. But first must he suffer many things and be rejected of this generation.

"And as it came to pass in the days of Noah, even so shall it be also in the days of the Son of man. They ate, they drank, they married, they were given in marriage, until the day that Noah entered into the ark, and the flood came, and destroyed them all. Likewise even as it came to pass in the days of Lot; they ate, they drank, they bought, they sold, they planted, they builded; but in the day that Lot went out from Sodom it rained fire and brimstone from heaven, and destroyed them all: after the same manner shall it be in the day that the Son of man is revealed. In that day, he that shall be on the housetop, and his goods in the house, let him not go down to take them away; and let him that is in the field likewise not return back. Remember Lot's wife. Whosoever shall seek to gain his life shall lose it; but whosoever shall lose his life shall preserve it."

THE UNJUST JUDGE.

And he spake a parable unto them to the end that they ought always to pray, and not to faint; saying, "There was in a city a judge, who feared not God, and regarded not man: and there was a widow in that city: and she came oft unto him, saying, 'Avenge me of mine adversary.' And he would not for a while: but afterward he said within himself, 'Though I fear not God, nor regard man; yet because this widow troubleth me, I will avenge her, lest she wear me out by her continual coming.'" And the Lord said, "Hear what the unrighteous judge saith. And shall not God avenge his elect, that cry to him day and night, and yet he is longsuffering over them? I say unto you, that he will avenge them speedily. Nevertheless, when the Son of man cometh, shall he find faith on the earth?"

THE PHARISEE AND THE PUBLICAN.

And he spake also this parable unto certain who trusted in themselves that they were righteous, and set all others at nought: "Two men went up into the temple to pray; the one a Pharisee, and the other a publican. The Pharisee stood and prayed thus with himself, 'God, I thank thee, that I am not as the rest of men, extortioners, unjust, adulterers, or even as this publican. I fast twice in the week; I give tithes of all that I get.' But the publican, standing afar off, would not lift up so much as his eyes unto heaven, but smote his breast, saying, 'God, be thou merciful to me a sinner.' I say unto you, This man went down to his house justified rather than the other: for every one that exalteth himself shall be humbled; but he that humbleth himself shall be exalted."

CONCERNING DIVORCE.

And there came unto him Pharisees, trying him, and saying, "Is it lawful for a man to put away his wife for every cause?"

And he answered and said, "Have ye not read, that he who made them from the beginning made them, male and female, and said, 'For this cause shall a man leave his father and mother, and shall cleave to his wife; and the two shall become one flesh?' So that they are no more two, but one flesh. What therefore God hath joined together, let not man put asunder."

They say unto him, "Why then did Moses command to give a bill of divorcement, and to put her away?"

He saith unto them, "Moses for your hardness of heart suffered you to put away your wives: but from the beginning it hath not been so. And I say unto you, Whosoever shall put away his wife, except for fornication, and shall marry another, committeth adultery: and he that marrieth her when she is put away committeth adultery."

The disciples say unto him, "If the case of the man is so with his wife, it is not expedient to marry."

But he said unto them, "Not all men can receive this saying, but they to whom it is given. For there are eunuchs, that were so born from their mother's womb: and there are eunuchs, that were made eunuchs by men: and there are eunuchs, that made themselves eunuchs for the kingdom of heaven's sake. He that is able to receive it, let him receive it."

JESUS AND THE CHILDREN.

And they were bringing unto him little children, that he should touch them: and the disciples rebuked them. But when Jesus saw it, he was moved with indignation, and said unto them, "Suffer the little children to come unto me; forbid them not: for to such belongeth the kingdom of God. Verily I say unto you, Whosoever shall not receive the kingdom of God as a little child, he shall in no wise enter therein."

And he took them in his arms, and blessed them, laying his hands upon them.

THE RICH YOUNG RULER.

And behold, as he was going forth into the way, a certain ruler ran to him, and kneeled to him, and asked him, "Good Teacher, what good thing shall I do that I may have eternal life?"

And he said unto him, "Why askest thou me concerning that which is good? None is good, save one, even God: but if thou wouldest enter into life, keep the commandments."

He saith unto him, "Which?"

And Jesus said, "Thou shalt not kill, Thou shalt not commit adultery, Thou shalt not steal, Thou shalt not bear false witness, Honor thy father and thy mother; and, Thou shalt love thy neighbor as thyself."

The young ruler saith unto him, "All these things have I observed from my youth up; what lack I yet?"

And Jesus, looking upon him, loved him, and said unto him, "One thing thou lackest yet: if thou wouldest be perfect, go, sell that which thou hast, and give to the poor, and thou shalt have treasure in heaven: and come, follow me."

But when the young man heard the saying, his countenance fell, and he went away sorrowful; for he was one that had great possessions.

And Jesus said unto his disciples, "Verily I say unto you, It is hard for a rich man to enter into the kingdom of heaven." And the disciples were amazed at his words. But Jesus answered again and said unto them, "Children, how hard it is for them that trust in riches to enter into the kingdom of God! It is easier for a camel to go through a needle's eye, than for a rich man to enter into the kingdom of God."

And when the disciples heard it, they were astonished exceedingly, saying, "Who then can be saved?"

And Jesus looking upon them said to them, "With men this is impossible: but with God all things are possible."

Then answered Peter and said unto him, "Lo, we have left all, and followed thee; what then shall we have?"

And Jesus said unto them, "Verily I say unto you, that ye who have followed me, in the regeneration when the Son of man shall sit on the throne of his glory, ye also shall sit upon twelve thrones, judging the twelve tribes of Israel. And every one that hath left houses, or brethren, or sisters, or father, or mother, or children, or lands, for my name's sake, shall receive a hundredfold now in this time, houses, and brethren, and sisters, and mothers, and children, and lands, with persecutions, and in the world to come shall inherit eternal life. But many shall be last that are first; and first that are last.

THE PARABLE OF THE VINEYARD.

"For the kingdom of heaven is like unto a man that was a householder, who went out early in the morning to hire laborers into his vineyard. And when he had agreed with the laborers for a shilling a day, he sent them into his vineyard. And he went out about the third hour, and saw others standing in the market-place idle; and to them he said, 'Go ye also into the vineyard, and whatsoever is right I will give you.' And they went their way. Again he went out about the sixth and the ninth hour, and did likewise. And about the eleventh hour he went out, and found others standing; and he saith unto them, 'Why stand ye here all the day idle?' They say unto him, 'Because no man hath hired us.' He saith unto them, 'Go ye also into the vineyard.' And when even was come, the lord of the vineyard saith unto his steward, 'Call the laborers and pay them their hire, beginning from the last unto the first.' And when they came that were hired about the eleventh hour, they received every man a shilling. And when the first came, they supposed that they would receive more; and they likewise received every man a shilling. And when they received it, they murmured against the householder, saying, 'These last have spent but one hour, and thou hast made them equal unto us, who have borne the burden of the day and the scorching heat.' But he answered and said to one of them, 'Friend, I do thee no wrong: didst not thou agree with me for a shilling? Take up that which is thine, and go thy way; it is my will to give unto this last, even as unto thee. Is it not lawful for me to do what I will with mine own? or is thine eye evil, because I am good?' So the last shall be first, and the first last."

THE LAST JOURNEY TO JERUSALEM
THE SHADOW OF THE CROSS.

And they were on the way, going up to Jerusalem; and Jesus was going before them: and they were amazed; and they that followed were afraid. And he took again the twelve, and began to tell them the things that were to happen unto him, saying, "Behold, we go up to Jerusalem; and all the things that are written by the prophets shall be accomplished unto the Son of man; and he shall be delivered unto the chief priests and the scribes; and they shall condemn him to death, and shall deliver him unto the Gentiles: and they shall mock him, and shall spit upon him, and shall scourge him, and shall kill him; and after three days he shall rise again."

And they understood none of these things: and this saying was hid from them: and they perceived not the things that were said.

THE SONS OF THUNDER.

Then came to him the mother of the sons of Zebedee with her sons James and John, worshipping him, and asking a certain thing of him.

And he said unto her, "What wouldest thou?"

She saith unto him, "Command that these my two sons may sit, one on thy right hand, and one on thy left hand, in thy kingdom."

But Jesus answered and said, "Ye know not what ye ask. Are ye able to drink the cup that I am about to drink? or to be baptized with the baptism that I am baptized with?"

And they said unto him, "We are able."

And Jesus said unto them, "The cup that I drink ye shall drink; and with the baptism that I am baptized withal shall ye be baptized: but to sit on my right hand or on my left hand is not mine to give; but it is for them for whom it hath been prepared of my Father."

And when the ten heard it, they began to be moved with indignation concerning James and John.

And Jesus called them to him, and saith unto them, "Ye know that they who are accounted to rule over the Gentiles lord it over them; and their great ones exercise authority over them. But it is not so among you: but whosoever would become great among you, shall be your minister; and whosoever would be first among you, shall be servant of all. Even as the Son of man also came not to be ministered unto, but to minister, and to give his life a ransom for many."

THE BLIND MAN OF JERICHO.

And they come to Jericho: and as they went out from Jericho, with his disciples and a great multitude, the son of Timaeus, Bartimaeus, a blind beggar, was sitting by the wayside, begging. And hearing the multitude going by, he inquired what this meant, and they told him that Jesus of Nazareth passeth by. And when he heard that it was Jesus the Nazarene, he began to cry out and say, "Jesus, thou son of David, have mercy on me."

And Jesus stood still, and said, "Call ye him."

And they call the blind man, saying unto him, "Be of good cheer: rise, he calleth thee." And he, casting away his garment, sprang up, and came to Jesus.

And Jesus answered him, and said, "What wilt thou that I should do unto thee?"

And the blind man said unto him, "Rabboni, that I may receive my sight."

And Jesus said unto him, "Go thy way; thy faith hath made thee whole."

And straightway he received his sight, and followed him in the way, glorifying God. And all the people, when they saw it, gave praise unto God.

THE VISIT TO ZACCHAEUS.

And he entered and was passing through Jericho. And behold, a man called by name Zacchaeus; and he was a chief publican, and he was rich. And he sought to see Jesus who he was; and could not for the crowd, because he was little of stature. And he ran on before, and climbed up into a sycamore tree to see him: for he was to pass that way.

And when Jesus came to the place, he looked up, and said unto him, "Zacchaeus, make haste, and come down; for to-day I must abide at thy house."

And he made haste, and came down, and received him joyfully.

And when they saw it, they all murmured, saying, "He is gone in to lodge with a man that is a sinner."

And Zacchaeus stood, and said unto the Lord, "Behold, Lord, the half of my goods I give to the poor; and if I have wrongfully exacted aught of any man, I restore fourfold."

And Jesus said unto him, "To-day is salvation come to this house, forasmuch as he also is a son of Abraham. For the Son of man came to seek and to save that which was lost."

THE PARABLE OF THE POUNDS.

And as they heard these things, he added and spake a parable, because he was nigh to Jerusalem, and because they supposed that the kingdom of God was immediately to appear. He said therefore, "A certain nobleman went into a far country, to receive for himself a kingdom, and to return. And he called ten servants of his, and gave them ten pounds, and said unto them, 'Trade ye herewith till I come.' But his citizens hated him, and sent an ambassage after him, saying, 'We will not that this man reign over us.'

"And it came to pass, when he was come back again, having received the kingdom, that he commanded these servants, unto whom he had given the money, to be called to him, that he might know what they had gained by trading. And the first came before him, saying, 'Lord, thy pound hath made ten pounds more.' And he said unto him, 'Well done, thou good servant: because thou wast found faithful in a very little, have thou authority over ten cities.' And the second came, saying, 'Thy pound, Lord, hath made five pounds.' And he said unto him also, 'Be thou also over five cities.' And another came, saying, 'Lord, behold, here is thy pound, which I kept laid up in a napkin: for I feared thee, because thou art an austere man: thou takest up that which thou layedst not down, and reapest that which thou didst not sow.' He saith unto him, 'Out of thine own mouth will I judge thee, thou wicked servant. Thou knewest that I am an austere man, taking up that which I laid not down, and reaping that which I did not sow; then wherefore gavest thou not my money into the bank, and I at my coming should have required it with interest?' And he said unto them that stood by, 'Take away from him the pound, and give it unto him that hath the ten pounds.' And they said unto him, 'Lord, he hath ten pounds.' 'I say unto you, that unto every one that hath shall be given; but from him that hath not, even that which he hath shall be taken away from him. But these mine enemies, that would not that I should reign over them, bring hither, and slay them before me.'"

And when he had thus spoken, he went on before, going up to Jerusalem.

GOING UP TO JERUSALEM.

Now the passover of the Jews was at hand: and many went up to Jerusalem out of the country before the passover, to purify themselves. They sought therefore for Jesus, and spake one with another, as they stood in the temple, "What think ye? That he will not come to the feast?"

Now the chief priests and the Pharisees had given commandment, that, if any man knew where he was, he should show it, that they might take him.

THE FEAST AT BETHANY.

Jesus therefore six days before the passover came to Bethany, where Lazarus was, whom Jesus raised from the dead. So they made him a supper there in the house of Simon the leper; and Martha served: but Lazarus was one of them that sat at meat with him. Mary therefore took a pound of ointment of pure nard, very precious, and anointed the feet of Jesus, and wiped his feet with her hair; and the house was filled with the odor of the ointment.

But Judas Iscariot, one of his disciples, that should betray him, saith, "Why was not this ointment sold for three hundred shillings, and given to the poor?"

Now this he said, not because he cared for the poor; but because he was a thief, and having the bag took away what was put therein.

Jesus therefore said, "Suffer her to keep it against the day of my burying. For the poor ye have always with you; but me ye have not always. She hath done what she could; she hath anointed my body beforehand for the burying. And verily I say unto you, Wheresoever the gospel shall be preached throughout the whole world, that also which this woman hath done shall be spoken of for a memorial of her."

The common people therefore of the Jews learned that he was there: and they came, not for Jesus' sake only, but that they might see Lazarus also, whom he had raised from the dead. But the chief priests took counsel that they might put Lazarus also to death; because that by reason of him many of the Jews went away, and believed on Jesus.

=HIS LAST WEEK=

PALM SUNDAY--THE DAY OF TRIUMPH
THE TRIUMPHAL ENTRY.

On the morrow when they drew nigh unto Jerusalem, unto Bethphage and Bethany, at the mount of Olives, he sendeth two of his disciples, and saith unto them, "Go your way into the village that is over against you: and straightway as ye enter into it, ye shall find a colt tied, whereon no man ever yet sat; loose him, and bring him. And if any one say unto you, 'Why do ye this?' say ye, 'The Lord hath need of him'; and straightway he will send him back hither."

Now this is come to pass, that it might be fulfilled, which was spoken through the prophet, saying,

"Tell ye the daughter of Zion, Behold, thy King cometh unto thee, Meek, and riding upon an ass, And upon a colt the foal of an ass."

And they went away, and found a colt tied at the door without in the open street: and they loose him. And certain of them that stood there said unto them, "What do ye, loosing the colt?" And they said unto them even as Jesus had said: and they let them go. And they bring the colt unto Jesus, and cast on him their garments; and he sat upon him.

And the most part of the multitude spread their garments upon the way; and others branches, which they had cut from the fields. And as he was drawing nigh, even at the descent of the Mount of Olives, the whole multitude of the disciples began to rejoice and praise God with a loud voice for all the mighty works which they had seen. And they that went before, and they that followed, cried, "Hosanna to the Son of David; Blessed is he that cometh in the name of the Lord; Blessed is the kingdom that cometh, the kingdom of our father David: Hosanna in the highest."

These things understood not his disciples at the first: but when Jesus was glorified, then remembered they that these things were written of him, and that they had done these things unto him.

The multitude, therefore, that was with him when he called Lazarus out of the tomb, and raised him from the dead, bare witness. For this cause also the multitude went and met him, for that they heard that he had done this sign.

And some of the Pharisees from the multitude said unto him, "Teacher, rebuke thy disciples."

And he answered and said, "I tell you that, if these shall hold their peace, the stones will cry out."

And when he drew nigh, he saw the city and wept over it, saying, "If thou hadst known in this day, even thou, the things which belong unto peace! but now they are hid from thine eyes. For the days shall come upon thee, when thine enemies shall cast up a bank about thee, and compass thee round, and keep thee in on every side, and shall dash thee to the ground, and thy children within thee: and they shall not leave in thee one stone upon another; because thou knewest not the time of thy visitation."

And when he was come into Jerusalem, all the city was stirred, saying, "Who is this?"

And the multitudes said, "This is the prophet, Jesus, from Nazareth of Galilee."

The Pharisees therefore said among themselves, "Behold, how ye prevail nothing; lo, the world is gone after him."

And he entered into Jerusalem, into the temple; and when he had looked round about upon all things, it being now eventide, he went out unto Bethany with the twelve.

MONDAY--THE DAY OF AUTHORITY
THE CURSING OF THE FIG TREE.

And on the morrow, when they were come out from Bethany, he hungered. And seeing a fig tree afar off having leaves, he came, if haply he might find anything thereon: and when he came to it, he found nothing but leaves; for it was not the season of figs. And he answered and said unto it, "No man eat fruit from thee henceforward for ever."

And his disciples heard it.

THE CLEANSING OF THE TEMPLE.

And they come to Jerusalem: and he entered into the temple, and began to cast out them that sold and them that bought in the temple, and overthrew the tables of the money-changers, and the seats of them that sold the doves: and he would not suffer that any man should carry a vessel through the temple. And he taught, and said unto them, "Is it not written, 'My house shall be called a house of prayer for all the nations?' but ye have made it a den of robbers?"

And the blind and the lame came to him in the temple; and he healed them. But when the chief priests and the scribes saw the wonderful things that he did, and the children that were crying in the temple and saying, "Hosanna to the son of David": they were moved with indignation, and said unto him, "Hearest thou what these are saying?"

And Jesus saith unto them, "Yea: did ye never read, 'Out of the mouth of babes and sucklings thou hast perfected praise'?"

And the chief priests and the scribes and the principal men of the people sought to destroy him: and they could not find what they might do; for the people all hung upon him, listening.

And he left them, and went forth out of the city to Bethany, and lodged there.

TUESDAY--THE DAY OF CONTROVERSY
THE LESSON FROM THE WITHERED FIG TREE.

And as they passed by in the morning, they saw the fig tree withered away from the roots. And Peter calling to remembrance saith unto him, "Rabbi, behold the fig tree which thou cursedst is withered away."

And Jesus answering saith unto them, "Have faith in God. Verily I say unto you, Whosoever shall say unto this mountain, 'Be thou taken up and cast into the sea'; and shall not doubt in his heart, but shall believe that what he saith cometh to pass; he shall have it. Therefore I say unto you, All things whatsoever ye pray and ask for, believe that ye receive them, and ye shall have them. And whensoever ye stand praying, forgive, if ye have aught against any one; that your Father also who is in heaven may forgive you your trespasses."

THE CHALLENGE OF CHRIST'S AUTHORITY.

And they came again to Jerusalem. And all the people came early in the morning to him in the temple to hear him. And as he was teaching the people in the temple, and preaching the gospel, there came upon him the chief priests and the scribes with the elders; and they spake, saying unto him, "Tell us: By what authority doest thou these things? or who is he that gave thee this authority?"

And Jesus answered, and said unto them, "I also will ask you one question, which if ye tell me, I likewise will tell you by what authority I do these things. The baptism of John, whence was it? from heaven or from men?"

And they reasoned with themselves, saying, "If we shall say, 'From heaven'; he will say unto us, 'Why did ye not believe him?' But if we shall say, 'From men'; all the people will stone us: for they are persuaded that John was a prophet."

And they answered Jesus, and said, "We know not."

And Jesus said unto them, "Neither tell I you by what authority I do these things."

THREE WARNING PARABLES. THE TWO SONS.

"But what think ye? A man had two sons; and he came to the first, and said, 'Son, go work to-day in the vineyard.' And he answered and said, 'I will not': but afterward he repented himself, and went. And he came to the second, and said likewise. And he answered and said, 'I go, sir': and went not. Which of the two did the will of his father?"

They say, "The first."

Jesus saith unto them, "Verily I say unto you, that the publicans and the harlots go into the kingdom of God before you. For John came unto you in the way of righteousness, and ye believed him not; but the publicans and the harlots believed him: and ye, when ye saw it, did not even repent yourselves afterward that ye might believe him."

THE WICKED HUSBANDMEN.

"Hear another parable: There was a man who was a householder, who planted a vineyard, and set a hedge about it, and digged a winepress in it, and built a tower, and let it out to husbandmen, and went into another country. And when the season of the fruits drew near, he sent his servants to the husbandmen, to receive his fruits. And the husbandmen took his servants, and beat one, and killed another, and stoned another. Again, he sent other servants more than the first: and they did unto them in like manner. But afterward he sent unto them his son, saying, 'They will reverence my son.' But the husbandmen, when they saw the son, said among themselves, 'This is the heir; come, let us kill him, and take his inheritance.' And they took him, and cast him forth out of the vineyard, and killed him. When therefore the lord of the vineyard shall come, what will he do unto those husbandmen?"

They say unto him, "He will miserably destroy those miserable men, and will let out the vineyard unto other husbandmen, who shall render him the fruits in their seasons."

Jesus saith unto them, "Did ye never read in the scriptures,

'The stone which the builders rejected,   The same was made the head of the corner;   This was from the Lord,   And it is marvellous in our eyes'?

"Therefore say I unto you, The kingdom of God shall be taken away from you, and shall be given to a nation bringing forth the fruits thereof. And he that falleth on this stone shall be broken to pieces; but on whomsoever it shall fall, it will scatter him as dust."

And when the chief priests and the Pharisees heard his parables, they perceived that he spake of them. And when they sought to lay hold on him, they feared the multitudes, because they took him for a prophet.

THE MARRIAGE OF THE KING'S SON.

And Jesus answered and spake again in parables unto them, saying, "The kingdom of heaven is likened unto a certain king, who made a marriage feast for his son, and sent forth his servants to call them that were bidden to the marriage feast: and they would not come. Again he sent forth other servants, saying, Tell them that are bidden, 'Behold, I have made ready my dinner; my oxen and my fatlings are killed, and all things are ready; come to the marriage feast.' But they made light of it, and went their ways, one to his own farm, another to his merchandise; and the rest laid hold on his servants, and treated them shamefully, and killed them. But the king was wroth; and he sent his armies, and destroyed those murderers, and burned their city. Then saith he to his servants, 'The wedding is ready, but they that were bidden were not worthy. Go ye therefore unto the partings of the highways, and as many as ye shall find, bid to the marriage feast.' And those servants went out into the highways, and gathered together all as many as they found, both bad and good; and the wedding was filled with guests. But when the king came in to behold the guests, he saw there a man who had not on a wedding-garment: and he saith unto him, 'Friend, how earnest thou in hither not having a wedding-garment?' And he was speechless. Then the king said to the servants, 'Bind him hand and foot and cast him out into the outer darkness'; there shall be the weeping and the gnashing of teeth. For many are called, but few chosen."

THREE HOSTILE QUESTIONS ASKED OF JESUS. TRIBUTE TO CAESAR.

Then went the Pharisees, and took counsel how they might ensnare him in his talk so as to deliver him up to the rule and to the authority of the governor. And they send to him their disciples, with the Herodians, saying, "Teacher, we know that thou art true, and teachest the way of God in truth, and carest not for any one: for thou regardest not the person of men. Tell us therefore, What thinkest thou? Is it lawful to give tribute unto Caesar, or not?"

But Jesus perceived their craftiness, and said, "Why make ye trial of me, ye hypocrites? Show me the tribute money."

And they brought unto him a denarius. And he saith unto them, "Whose is this image and superscription?"

They say unto him, "Caesar's."

Then he saith unto them, "Render therefore unto Caesar the things that are Caesar's; and unto God the things that are God's."

And when they heard it, they marvelled, and left him, and went away.

THE QUESTION OF THE RESURRECTION.

And there came to him certain of the Sadducees, they that say that there is no resurrection; and they asked him, saying, "Teacher, Moses wrote unto us, that if a man's brother die, having a wife, and he be childless, his brother should take the wife, and raise up seed unto his brother. There were therefore seven brethren: and the first took a wife, and died childless; and the second; and the third took her; and likewise the seven also left no children, and died. Afterward the woman also died. In the resurrection therefore whose wife of them shall she be? for the seven had her to wife."

And Jesus said unto them, "Ye do err, not knowing the scriptures, nor the power of God. The sons of this world marry, and are given in marriage: but they that are accounted worthy to attain to that world, and the resurrection from the dead, neither marry, nor are given in marriage: for neither can they die any more: for they are equal unto the angels; and are sons of God, being sons of the resurrection. But that the dead are raised, even Moses showed, in the place concerning the Bush, when he calleth the Lord the God of Abraham, and the God of Isaac, and the God of Jacob. Now he is not the God of the dead but of the living: for all live unto him."

And when the multitudes heard it, they were astonished at his teaching.

THE GREATEST COMMANDMENT.

And one of the scribes came, and heard them questioning together, and knowing that he had answered them well, asked him, "What commandment is the first of all?"

Jesus answered, "The first is, 'Hear, O Israel: The Lord our God, the Lord is one: and thou shalt love the Lord thy God with all thy heart, and with all thy soul, and with all thy mind, and with all thy strength.' The second is this, 'Thou shalt love thy neighbor as thyself.' There is none other commandment greater than these."

And the scribe said unto him, "Of a truth, Teacher, thou hast well said that he is one: and there is none other but he: and to love him with all the heart, and with all the understanding and with all the strength, and to love his neighbor as himself, is much more than all whole burnt-offerings and sacrifices."

And when Jesus saw that he answered discreetly, he said unto him, "Thou art not far from the kingdom of God."

THE UNANSWERABLE QUESTION OF JESUS.

Now while the Pharisees were gathered together Jesus asked them a question, saying, "What think ye of the Christ? whose son is he?"

They say unto him, "The son of David."

He saith unto them, "How then doth David in the Spirit call him Lord, saying,

'The Lord said unto my Lord,   Sit thou on my right hand,   Till I put thine enemies underneath thy feet'?

If David then calleth him Lord, how is he his son?"

And no one was able to answer him a word, neither durst any man from that day forth ask him any more questions.

And the common people heard him gladly.

DISCOURSE OF JESUS AGAINST THE SCRIBES AND PHARISEES.

Then spake Jesus to the multitudes and to his disciples, saying, "The scribes and the Pharisees sit on Moses' seat: all things therefore whatsoever they bid you, these do and observe: but do not ye after their works; for they say, and do not. Yea, they bind heavy burdens and grievous to be borne, and lay them on men's shoulders; but they themselves will not move them with their finger. But all their works they do to be seen of men: for they make broad their phylacteries, and enlarge the borders of their garments, and love the chief place at feasts, and the chief seats in the synagogues, and the salutations in the marketplaces, and to be called of men, 'Rabbi.' But be not ye called 'Rabbi,' for one is your teacher, and all ye are brethren. And call no man your father on the earth: for one is your Father, even he who is in heaven. Neither be ye called masters: for one is your master, even the Christ. But he that is greatest among you shall be your servant. And whosoever shall exalt himself shall be humbled: and whosoever shall humble himself shall be exalted.

"But woe unto you, scribes and Pharisees, hypocrites! because ye shut the kingdom of heaven against men: for ye enter not in yourselves, neither suffer ye them that are entering in to enter.

"Woe unto you, scribes and Pharisees, hypocrites! for ye compass sea and land to make one proselyte; and when he is become so, ye make him twofold more a son of hell than yourselves.

"Woe unto you, ye blind guides, that say, 'Whosoever shall swear by the temple, it is nothing; but whosoever shall swear by the gold of the temple, he is a debtor.' Ye fools and blind: for which is greater, the gold, or the temple that hath sanctified the gold? And, 'Whosoever shall swear by the altar, it is nothing; but whosoever shall swear by the gift that is upon it, he is a debtor.' Ye blind: for which is greater, the gift, or the altar that sanctifieth the gift? He therefore that sweareth by the altar, sweareth by it, and by all things thereon. And he that sweareth by the temple, sweareth by it, and by him that dwelleth therein. And he that sweareth by the heaven, sweareth by the throne of God, and by him that sitteth thereon.

"Woe unto you, scribes and Pharisees, hypocrites! for ye tithe mint and anise and cummin, and have left undone the weightier matters of the law, justice, and mercy, and faith: but these ye ought to have done, and not to have left the other undone. Ye blind guides that strain out the gnat, and swallow the camel!

"Woe unto you, scribes and Pharisees, hypocrites! for ye cleanse the outside of the cup and of the platter, but within they are full from extortion and excess. Thou blind Pharisee, cleanse first the inside of the cup and of the platter, that the outside thereof may become clean also.

"Woe unto you, scribes and Pharisees, hypocrites! for ye are like unto whited sepulchres, which outwardly appear beautiful, but inwardly are full of dead men's bones, and of all uncleanness. Even so ye also outwardly appear righteous unto men, but inwardly ye are full of hypocrisy and iniquity.

"Woe unto you, scribes and Pharisees, hypocrites! for ye build the sepulchres of the prophets, and garnish the tombs of the righteous, and say, 'If we had been in the days of our fathers, we should not have been partakers with them in the blood of the prophets.' Wherefore ye witness to yourselves, that ye are sons of them that slew the prophets. Fill ye up then the measure of your fathers. Ye serpents, ye offspring of vipers, how shall ye escape the judgment of hell? Therefore, behold, I send unto you prophets, and wise men, and scribes: some of them shall ye kill and crucify; and some of them shall ye scourge in your synagogues, and persecute from city to city: that upon you may come all the righteous blood shed on the earth, from the blood of Abel the righteous unto the blood of Zachariah son of Barachiah, whom ye slew between the sanctuary and the altar. Verily I say unto you, All these things shall come upon this generation.

"O Jerusalem, Jerusalem, that killeth the prophets, and stoneth them that are sent unto her! how often would I have gathered thy children together, even as a hen gathereth her chickens under her wings, and ye would not! Behold, your house is left unto you desolate. For I say unto you, Ye shall not see me henceforth, till ye shall say, 'Blessed is he that cometh in the name of the Lord.'"

THE WIDOW'S TWO MITES.

And he sat down over against the treasury, and beheld how the multitude cast money into the treasury: and many that were rich cast in much. And there came a poor widow, and she cast in two mites, which make a farthing. And he called unto him his disciples, and said unto them, "Verily, I say unto you, This poor widow cast in more than all they that are casting into the treasury: for they all did cast in of their superfluity; but she of her want did cast in all that she had, even all her living."

THE GENTILES SEEK JESUS.

Now there were certain Greeks among those that went up to worship at the feast: these therefore came to Philip, who was of Bethsaida of Galilee, and asked him, saying, "Sir, we would see Jesus."

Philip cometh and telleth Andrew: Andrew cometh, and Philip, and they tell Jesus.

And Jesus answereth them, saying, "The hour is come, that the Son of man should be glorified. Verily, verily, I say unto you, Except a grain of wheat fall into the earth and die, it abideth by itself alone; but if it die, it beareth much fruit. He that loveth his life loseth it: and he that hateth his life in this world shall keep it unto life eternal. If any man serve me, let him follow me: and where I am, there shall also my servant be: if any man serve me, him will the Father honor. Now is my soul troubled; and what shall I say? Father, save me from this hour. But for this cause came I unto this hour. Father, glorify thy name."

There came therefore a voice out of heaven, saying, "I have both glorified it, and will glorify it again."

The multitude, therefore, that stood by, and heard it, said that it had thundered: others said, "An angel hath spoken to him."

Jesus answered and said, "This voice hath not come for my sake, but for your sakes. Now is the judgment of this world: now shall the prince of this world be cast out. And I, if I be lifted up from the earth, will draw all men unto myself."

But this he said, signifying by what manner of death he should die.

The multitude therefore answered him, "We have heard out of the law that the Christ abideth forever; and how sayest thou, 'The Son of man must be lifted up'? who is this Son of man?"

Jesus therefore said unto them, "Yet a little while is the light among you. Walk while ye have the light, that darkness overtake you not; and he that walketh in the darkness knoweth not whither he goeth. While ye have the light, believe on the light, that ye may become sons of light."

These things spake Jesus, and he departed and hid himself from them.

THE JEWS REJECT JESUS.

But though he had done so many signs before them, yet they believed not on him: that the word of Isaiah the prophet might be fulfilled, which he spake,

> "Lord, who hath believed our report?
> And to whom hath the arm of the Lord been revealed?"

For this cause they could not believe, for that Isaiah said again.

> "He hath blinded their eyes, and he hardened their heart;
> Lest they should see with their eyes, and perceive with their
>   heart,
> And should turn,
> And I should heal them."

These things said Isaiah, because he saw his glory; and he spake of him. Nevertheless even of the rulers many believed on him; but because of the Pharisees they did not confess it, lest they should be put out of the synagogue; for they loved the glory that is of men more than the glory that is of God.

And Jesus cried and said, "He that believeth on me, believeth not on me, but on him that sent me. And he that beholdeth me beholdeth him that sent me. I am come a light into the world, that whosoever believeth on me may not abide in the darkness. And if any man hear my sayings, and keep them not, I judge him not: for I came not to judge the world, but to save the world. He that rejecteth me, and receiveth not my sayings, hath one that judgeth him: the word that I spake, the same shall judge him in the last day. For I spake not from myself; but the Father that sent me, he hath given me a commandment, what I should say, and what I should speak. And I know that his commandment is life eternal; the things therefore which I speak, even as the Father hath said unto me, so I speak."

DISCOURSE CONCERNING THE FUTURE.

And Jesus went out from the temple, and was going on his way; and his disciples came to him to show him the buildings of the temple.

But he answered and said unto them, "See ye not all these things? Verily I say unto you, There shall not be left here one stone upon another, that shall not be thrown down."

And as he sat on the mount of Olives over against the temple, Peter and James and John and Andrew asked him privately, "Tell us, when shall these things be? and what shall be the sign when these things are all about to be accomplished?"

And Jesus began to say unto them, "Take heed that no man lead you astray. Many shall come in my name, saying, 'I am he,' and shall lead many astray. And when ye shall hear of wars and rumors of wars, be not troubled: these things must needs come to pass; but the end is not yet. For nation shall rise against nation, and kingdom against kingdom; there shall be earthquakes in divers places; there shall be famines: these things are the beginning of the travail.

"But take ye heed to yourselves: for they shall deliver you up to councils; and in synagogues shall ye be beaten; and before governors and kings shall ye stand for my sake, for a testimony unto them. And the gospel must first be preached unto all the nations. And when they lead you to judgment, and deliver you up, be not anxious beforehand what ye shall speak; but whatsoever shall be given you in that hour, that speak ye; for it is not ye that speak, but the Holy Spirit. But ye shall be delivered up even by parents, and brethren, and kinsfolk, and friends: and some of you shall they cause to be put to death And ye shall be hated of all men for my name's sake.

"And then shall many stumble, and shall deliver up one another, and shall hate one another. And many false prophets shall arise, and shall lead many astray. And because iniquity shall be multiplied, the love of the many shall wax cold. But he that endureth to the end, the same shall be saved.

"But when ye see Jerusalem compassed with armies, then know that her desolation is at hand. Then let them that are in Judaea flee unto the mountains: let him that is on the housetop not go down to take out the things that are in his house: and let him that is in the field not return back to take his cloak. For these are days of vengeance, that all things which are written may be fulfilled.

"But woe unto them that are with child and to them that give suck in those days! And pray ye that your flight be not in the winter, neither on a Sabbath: for then shall be great tribulation, such as hath not been from the beginning of the world until now, no, nor ever shall be. And except those days had been shortened, no flesh would have been saved: but for the elect's sake those days shall be shortened. Then if any man shall say unto you, 'Lo, here is the Christ,' or, 'Here,' believe it not. For there shall arise false Christs, and false prophets, and shall show great signs and wonders; so as to lead astray, if possible, even the elect. But take ye heed: behold, I have told you all things beforehand. If, therefore, they shall say unto you, 'Behold, he is in the wilderness,' go not forth: 'Behold, he is in the inner chambers,' believe it not. For as the lightning cometh forth from the east and is seen even unto the west, so shall be the coming of the Son of man. Wheresoever the carcase is, there will the eagles be gathered together.

"But immediately after the tribulation of those days the sun shall be darkened, and the moon shall not give her light, and the stars shall fall from heaven, and the powers of the heavens shall be shaken: and then shall appear the sign of the Son of man in heaven: and then shall all the tribes of the earth mourn, and they shall see the Son of man coming on the clouds of heaven with power and great glory. And he shall send forth his angels with a great sound of a trumpet, and shall gather together his elect from the four winds, from the uttermost part of the earth to the uttermost part of heaven.

"Now from the fig tree learn her parable: when her branch is now become tender, and putteth forth its leaves, ye know that the summer is nigh; even so ye also, when ye see all these things, know ye that he is nigh, even at the doors. Verily I say unto you, This generation shall not pass away till all these things be accomplished. Heaven and earth shall pass away, but my words shall not pass away. But of that day and hour knoweth no one, not even the angels of heaven, neither the Son, but the Father only.

"But take heed to yourselves, lest haply your hearts be overcharged with surfeiting, and drunkenness, and cares of this life, and that day come on you suddenly as a snare; for so shall it come upon all them that dwell on the face of all the earth. But watch ye at every season, making supplication, that ye may prevail to escape all these things that shall come to pass, and to stand before the Son of man.

"And as were the days of Noah, so shall be the coming of the Son of man. For as in those days which were before the flood they were eating and drinking, marrying and giving in marriage, until the day that Noah entered into the ark, and they knew not until the flood came, and took them all away; so shall be the coming of the Son of man. Then shall two men be in the field; one is taken, and one is left; two women shall be grinding at the mill: one is taken, and one is left. Watch therefore: for ye know not on what day your Lord cometh.

"But know this, that if the master of the house had known in what watch the thief was coming, he would have watched, and would not have suffered his house to be broken through. Therefore be ye also ready; for in an hour that ye think not the Son of man cometh.

"Take ye heed, watch and pray: for ye know not when the time is. It is as when a man, sojourning in another country, having left his house, and given authority to his servants, to each one his work, commanded also the porter to watch. Watch therefore: for ye know not when the lord of the house cometh, whether at even, or at midnight, or at cockcrowing, or in the morning; lest coming suddenly he find you sleeping. And what I say unto you I say unto all, Watch.

"Who then is the faithful and wise servant, whom the lord hath set over his household, to give them their food in due season? Blessed is that servant, whom his lord when he cometh shall find so doing. Verily I say unto you, that he will set him over all that he hath. But if that evil servant shall say in his heart, 'My lord tarrieth;' and shall begin to beat his fellow-servants, and shall eat and drink with the drunken; the lord of that servant shall come in a day when he expecteth not, and in an hour when he knoweth not, and shall cut him asunder, and appoint his portion with the hypocrites: there shall be the weeping and the gnashing of teeth."

THREE LESSONS TO THE DISCIPLES. THE PARABLE OF THE TEN VIRGINS.

"Then shall the kingdom of heaven be likened unto ten virgins, who took their lamps and went forth to meet the bridegroom. And five of them were foolish, and five were wise. For the foolish, when they took their lamps, took no oil with them: but the wise took oil in their vessels with their lamps. Now while the bridegroom tarried, they all slumbered and slept. But at midnight there is a cry, 'Behold, the bridegroom! Come ye forth to meet him.' Then all those virgins arose, and trimmed their lamps. And the foolish said unto the wise, 'Give us of your oil; for our lamps are going out.' But the wise answered, saying, 'Peradventure there will not be enough for us and you: go ye rather to them that sell, and buy for yourselves.'

"And while they went away to buy, the bridegroom came; and they that were ready went in with him to the marriage feast: and the door was shut. Afterward came also the other virgins, saying, 'Lord, Lord, open to us.' But he answered and said, 'Verily I say unto you, I know you not.'

"Watch therefore, for ye know not the day nor the hour.

THE PARABLE OF THE TALENTS.

"For it is as when a man, going into another country, called his own servants, and delivered unto them his goods. And unto one he gave five talents, to another two, to another one; to each according to his several ability; and he went on his journey. Straightway he that received the five talents went and traded with them, and made other five talents. In like manner he also that received the two gained other two. But he that received the one went away and digged in the earth, and hid his lord's money.

"Now after a long time the lord of these servants cometh, and maketh a reckoning with them. And he that received the five talents came and brought other five talents, saying, 'Lord, thou deliveredst unto me five talents: lo, I have gained other five talents.' His lord said unto him, 'Well done, good and faithful servant: thou hast been faithful over a few things, I will set thee over many things; enter thou into the joy of thy lord.'

"And he also that received the two talents came and said, 'Lord, thou deliveredst unto me two talents: lo, I have gained other two talents.'

"His lord said unto him, 'Well done, good and faithful servant: thou hast been faithful over a few things, I will set thee over many things; enter thou into the joy of thy lord.'

"And he also that had received the one talent came and said, 'Lord, I knew thee that thou art a hard man, reaping where thou didst not sow, and gathering where thou didst not scatter; and I was afraid, and went away and hid thy talent in the earth: lo, thou hast thine own.'

"But his lord answered and said unto him, 'Thou wicked and slothful servant, thou knewest that I reap where I sowed not, and gather where I did not scatter; thou oughtest therefore to have put my money to the bankers, and at my coming I should have received back mine own with interest. Take ye away therefore the talent from him, and give it unto him that hath the ten talents. For unto every one that hath shall be given, and he shall have abundance; but from him that hath not, even that which he hath shall be taken away. And cast ye out the unprofitable servant into the outer darkness: there shall be the weeping and the gnashing of teeth.'

THE JUDGMENT SCENE.

"But when the Son of man shall come in his glory, and all the angels with him, then shall he sit on the throne of his glory: and before him shall be gathered all the nations: and he shall separate them one from another, as the shepherd separateth the sheep from the goats; and he shall set the sheep on his right hand, but the goats on the left. Then shall the King say unto them on his right hand, 'Come, ye blessed of my Father, inherit the kingdom prepared for you from the foundation of the world: for I was hungry, and ye gave me to eat; I was thirsty, and ye gave me drink; I was a stranger, and ye took me in; naked, and ye clothed me; I was sick, and ye visited me; I was in prison, and ye came unto me.'

"Then shall the righteous answer him, saying, 'Lord, when saw we thee hungry, and fed thee? or athirst, and gave thee drink? And when saw we thee a stranger, and took thee in? or naked, and clothed thee? And when saw we thee sick, or in prison, and came unto thee?' And the King shall answer and say unto them, 'Verily I say unto you, Inasmuch as ye did it unto one of these my children, even these least, ye did it unto me.'

"Then shall he say also unto them on the left hand, 'Depart from me, ye cursed, into the eternal fire which is prepared for the devil and his angels: for I was hungry, and ye did not give me to eat; I was thirsty, and ye gave me no drink; I was a stranger, and ye took me not in; naked, and ye clothed me not; sick, and in prison, and ye visited me not.' Then shall they also answer, saying, 'Lord, when saw we thee hungry, or athirst, or a stranger, or naked, or sick, or in prison, and did not minister unto thee?' Then shall he answer them, saying, 'Verily I say unto you, Inasmuch as ye did it not unto one of these least, ye did it not unto me.' And these shall go away into eternal punishment: but the righteous into eternal life."

THE CONSPIRACY AGAINST JESUS.

And it came to pass, when Jesus had finished all these words, he said unto his disciples, "Ye know that after two days the passover cometh, and the Son of man is delivered up to be crucified."

Then were gathered together the chief priests, the elders of the people, unto the court of the high priest, who was called Caiaphas; and they took counsel together that they might take Jesus by subtlety, and kill him. But they said, "Not during the feast, lest a tumult arise among the people."

And Satan entered into Judas, who was called Iscariot, being of the number of the twelve. And he went away and communed with the chief priests and captains, how he might deliver him unto them. And they were glad, and they weighed unto him thirty pieces of silver. And from that time he sought opportunity to deliver him unto them in the absence of the multitude.

WEDNESDAY--THE DAY OF RETIREMENT

[There is no record of the events of this day. Jesus spent it in retirement, almost certainly in the home of his friends at Bethany.]

THURSDAY--THE DAY OF FELLOWSHIP PREPARATION FOR THE PASSOVER.

And on the first day of unleavened bread, when they sacrificed the passover, his disciples say unto him, "Where wilt thou that we go and make ready that thou mayest eat the passover?"

And he sendeth two of his disciples, and saith unto them, "Go into the city, and there shall meet you a man bearing a pitcher of water; follow him; and wheresoever he shall enter in, say to the master of the house, 'The Teacher saith, My time is at hand. Where is my guest-chamber, where I shall eat the passover with my disciples?' And he will himself show you a large upper room furnished and ready: and there make ready for us."

And the disciples went forth, and came into the city, and found as he had said unto them: and they made ready the passover.

STRIFE AMONG THE DISCIPLES.

And when it was evening he cometh with the twelve. And there arose also a contention among them, which of them was accounted to be greatest. And he said unto them, "The kings of the Gentiles have lordship over them; and they that have authority over them are called Benefactors. But ye shall not be so: but he that is the greater among you, let him become as the younger: and he that is chief, as he that doth serve. For which is greater, he that sitteth at meat, or he that serveth? Is not he that sitteth at meat? But I am in the midst of you as he that serveth. But ye are they that have continued with me in my temptations; and I appoint unto you a kingdom, even as my Father appointed unto me, that ye may eat and drink at my table in my kingdom; and ye shall sit on thrones judging the twelve tribes of Israel."

JESUS WASHING THE DISCIPLES' FEET.

Now before the feast of the passover, Jesus knowing that his hour was come that he should depart out of this world unto the Father, having loved his own that were in the world, he loved them unto the end.

And during supper, the devil having already put into the heart of Judas Iscariot, Simon's son, to betray him, Jesus, knowing that the Father had given all things into his hands, and that he came forth from God, and goeth unto God, riseth from supper, and layeth aside his garments; and he took a towel, and girded himself. Then he poureth water into the basin, and began to wash the disciples' feet, and to wipe them with the towel wherewith he was girded.

So he cometh to Simon Peter. He saith unto him, "Lord, dost thou wash my feet?"

Jesus answered and said unto him, "What I do thou knowest not now; but thou shall understand hereafter."

Peter saith unto him, "Thou shalt never wash my feet."

Jesus answered him, "If I wash thee not, thou hast no part with me."

Simon Peter saith unto him, "Lord, not my feet only, but also my hands and my head."

Jesus saith to him, "He that is bathed needeth not save to wash his feet, but is clean every whit: and ye are clean, but not all." For he knew him that should betray him; therefore said he, "Ye are not all clean."

So when he had washed their feet, and taken his garments, and sat down again, he said unto them, "Know ye what I have done to you? Ye call me Teacher, and Lord: and ye say well; for so I am. If I then, the Lord and the Teacher, have washed your feet, ye also ought to wash one another's feet. For I have given you an example, that ye also should do as I have done to you. Verily, verily, I say unto you, A servant is not greater than his lord; neither one that is sent greater than he that sent him. If ye know these things, blessed are ye if ye do them.

"I speak not of you all: I know whom I have chosen: but that the scripture may be fulfilled, He that eateth my bread lifted up his heel against me. From henceforth I tell you before it come to pass, that, when it is come to pass, ye may believe that I am he. Verily, verily, I say unto you, He that receiveth whomsoever I send receiveth me; and he that receiveth me receiveth him that sent me."

THE BETRAYER POINTED OUT.

When Jesus had thus said, he was troubled in the spirit, and testified, and said, "Verily, verily, I say unto you, that one of you shall betray me."

The disciples looked one on another, doubting of whom he spake. And they were exceeding sorrowful, and began to say unto him every one, "Is it I, Lord?"

And he answered and said, "He that dipped his hand with me in the dish, the same shall betray me. The Son of man goeth, even as it is written of him: but woe unto that man through whom the Son of man is betrayed! Good were it for that man if he had not been born."

And Judas, who betrayed him, answered and said, "Is it I, Rabbi?"

He saith unto him, "Thou hast said."

There was at the table reclining in Jesus' bosom one of his disciples, whom Jesus loved. Simon Peter therefore beckoneth to him, and saith unto him, "Tell us who it is of whom he speaketh."

He leaning back, as he was, on Jesus' breast, saith unto him, "Lord, who is it?"

Jesus therefore answereth, "He it is, for whom I shall dip the sop, and give it him."

So when he had dipped the sop, he taketh and giveth it to Judas, the son of Simon Iscariot. And after the sop, then entered Satan into him.

Jesus therefore saith unto him, "What thou doest, do quickly."

Now no man at the table knew for what intent he spake this unto him. For some thought because Judas had the bag, that Jesus said unto him, "Buy what things we have need of for the feast," or that he should give something to the poor. He then having received the sop went out straightway: and it was night.

When therefore he was gone out, Jesus saith, "Now is the Son of man glorified, and God is glorified in him; and God shall glorify him in himself, and straightway shall he glorify him."

THE LORD'S SUPPER.

And he said unto them, "With desire I have desired to eat this passover with you before I suffer: for I say unto you, I shall not eat it until it be fulfilled in the Kingdom of God."

And he took bread, and when he had given thanks, he brake it, and gave to them, saying, "This is my body; which is given for you; this do in remembrance of me."

And he took a cup, in like manner after supper, and gave thanks, and gave to them, saying, "Drink ye all of it; for this is my blood of the new covenant, which is poured out for you, for many, unto remission of sins. Take this and divide it among yourselves; for I say unto you, I shall not drink from henceforth of the fruit of the vine, until the Kingdom of God shall come."

THE FAREWELL CONVERSATION.

"Little children, yet a little while I am with you. Ye shall seek me: and as I said unto the Jews, 'Whither I go, ye cannot come,' so now I say unto you. A new commandment I give unto you, that ye love one another; even as I have loved you, that ye also love one another. By this shall all men know that ye are my disciples, if ye have love one to another."

Simon Peter saith unto him, "Lord, whither goest thou?"

Jesus answered, "Whither I go, thou canst not follow me now; but thou shalt follow afterwards."

And Jesus saith unto them, "All ye shall be offended: for it is written, I will smite the shepherd, and the sheep shall be scattered abroad. Howbeit, after I am raised up, I will go before you into Galilee."

But Peter said unto him, "Although all shall be offended, yet will not I."

And Jesus saith unto him, "Verily I say unto thee, that thou to-day, even this night, before the cock crow twice, shalt deny me thrice. Simon, Simon, behold Satan asked to have you, that he might sift you as wheat: but I make supplication for thee, that thy faith fail not: and do thou, when once thou hast turned again, establish thy brethren."

But he spake vehemently, "If I must die with thee, I will not deny thee." And in like manner also said they all.

*   *   *   *   *

And he said unto them, "When I sent you forth without purse, and wallet, and shoes, lacked ye anything?"

And they said, "Nothing."

And he said unto them, "But now, he that hath a purse, let him take it, and likewise a wallet; and he that hath none, let him sell his cloak, and buy a sword. For I say unto you, that this which is written must be fulfilled in me, 'And he was reckoned with transgressors': for that which concerneth me hath fulfillment."

And they said, "Lord, behold, here are two swords."

And he said unto them, "It is enough."

*   *   *   *   *

"Let not your heart be troubled; believe in God, believe also in me. In my Father's house are many mansions; if it were not so, I would have told you; for I go to prepare a place for you. And if I go and prepare a place for you, I come again, and will receive you unto myself; that where I am, there ye may be also. And whither I go, ye know the way."

Thomas saith unto him, "Lord, we know not whither thou goest; how know we the way?"

Jesus saith unto him, "I am the way, and the truth, and the life: no one cometh unto the Father, but by me. If ye had known me, ye would have known my Father also: from henceforth ye know him, and have seen him."

Philip saith unto him, "Lord, show us the Father, and it sufficeth us."

Jesus saith unto him, "Have I been so long time with you, and dost thou not know me, Philip? He that hath seen me hath seen the Father: how sayest thou, 'Show us the Father?' Believest thou not that I am in the Father, and the Father in me? The words that I say unto you I speak not from myself: but the Father abiding in me doeth his works. Believe me that I am in the Father, and the Father in me: or else believe me for the very works' sake. Verily, verily, I say unto you, He that believeth on me, the works that I do shall he do also: and greater works than these shall he do; because I go unto the Father. And whatsoever ye shall ask in my name, that will I do, that the Father may be glorified in the Son. If ye shall ask anything in my name, that will I do. If ye love me, ye will keep my commandments. And I will pray the Father, and he shall give you another Comforter, that he may be with you for ever, even the Spirit of truth: whom the world cannot receive; for it beholdeth him not, neither knoweth him: ye know him, for he abideth with you, and shall be in you. I will not leave you desolate: I come unto you.

"Yet a little while, and the world beholdeth me no more; but ye behold me: because I live, ye shall live also. In that day ye shall know that I am in my Father, and ye in me, and I in you. He that hath my commandments, and keepeth them, he it is that loveth me: and he that loveth me shall be loved of my Father, and I will love him, and will manifest myself unto him."

Judas (not Iscariot) saith unto him, "Lord, what is come to pass that thou wilt manifest thyself unto us, and not unto the world?"

Jesus answered and said unto him, "If a man love me, he will keep my word: and my Father will love him, and we will come unto him, and make our abode with him. He that loveth me not keepeth not my words: and the word which ye hear is not mine, but the Father's who sent me.

"These things have I spoken unto you, while yet abiding with you. But the Comforter, even the Holy Spirit, whom the Father will send in my name, he shall teach you all things, and bring to your remembrance all that I said unto you. Peace I leave with you; my peace I give unto you: not as the world giveth, give I unto you. Let not your heart be troubled, neither let it be fearful. Ye heard how I said to you, I go away, and I come unto you. If ye loved me, ye would have rejoiced, because I go unto the Father: for the Father is greater than I.

"And now I have told you before it come to pass, that, when it is come to pass, ye may believe. I will no more speak much with you, for the prince of the world cometh: and he hath nothing in me; but that the world may know that I love the Father, and as the Father gave me commandment, even so I do."

*   *   *   *   *

"I am the true vine, and my Father is the husbandman. Every branch in me that beareth not fruit, he taketh it away: and every branch that beareth fruit, he cleanseth it, that it may bear more fruit. Already ye are clean because of the word which I have spoken unto you. Abide in me, and I in you. As the branch cannot bear fruit of itself, except it abide in the vine; so neither can ye, except ye abide in me. I am the vine, ye are the branches: He that abideth in me, and I in him, the same beareth much fruit: for apart from me ye can do nothing. If a man abide not in me, he is cast forth as a branch, and is withered; and they gather them, and cast them into the fire, and they are burned. If ye abide in me, and my words abide in you, ask whatsoever ye will, and it shall be done unto you. Herein is my Father glorified, that ye bear much fruit: and so shall ye be my disciples. Even as the Father hath loved me, I also have loved you: abide ye in my love. If ye keep my commandments, ye shall abide in my love; even as I have kept my Father's commandments, and abide in his love.

"These things have I spoken unto you, that my joy may be in you, and that your joy may be made full. This is my commandment, that ye love one another, even as I have loved you. Greater love hath no man than this, that a man lay down his life for his friends. Ye are my friends, if ye do the things which I command you. No longer do I call you servants; for the servant knoweth not what his lord doeth: but I have called you friends; for all things that I heard from my Father I have made known unto you. Ye did not choose me, but I chose you, and appointed you, that ye should go and bear fruit, and that your fruit should abide: that whatsoever ye shall ask of the Father in my name, he may give it you. These things I command you, that ye may love one another. If the world hated you, ye know that it hath hated me before it hated you. If ye were of the world, the world would love its own: but because ye are not of the world, but I chose you out of the world, therefore the world hateth you. Remember the word that I said unto you, A servant is not greater than his lord. If they persecuted me, they will also persecute you; if they kept my word, they will keep yours also. But all these things will they do unto you for my name's sake, because they know not him that sent me. If I had not come and spoken unto them, they had not had sin: but now they have no excuse for their sin. He that hateth me hateth my Father also. If I had not done among them the works which none other did, they had not had sin: but now have they both seen and hated me and my Father. But this cometh to pass, that the word may be fulfilled that is written in their law, 'They hated me without a cause.' But when the Comforter is come, whom I will send unto you from the Father, even the Spirit of truth, which proceedeth from the Father, he shall bear witness of me: and ye also bear witness, because ye have been with me from the beginning.

"These things have I spoken unto you, that ye should not be caused to stumble. They shall put you out of the synagogues: yea, the hour cometh, that whosoever killeth you shall think that he offereth service unto God. And these things will they do, because they have not known the Father, nor me. But these things have I spoken unto you, that when their hour is come, ye may remember them, how that I told you. And these things I said not unto you from the beginning, because I was with you. But now I go unto him that sent me; and none of you asketh me, 'Whither goest thou?' But because I have spoken these things unto you, sorrow hath filled your heart. Nevertheless I tell you the truth: It is expedient for you that I go away; for if I go not away, the Comforter will not come unto you; but if I go, I will send him unto you. And he, when he is come, will convict the world in respect of sin, and of righteousness, and of judgment: of sin, because they believe not on me; of righteousness, because I go to the Father, and ye behold me no more; of judgment, because the prince of this world hath been judged. I have yet many things to say unto you, but ye cannot bear them now. Howbeit when he, the Spirit of truth, is come, he shall guide you into all the truth: for he shall not speak from himself; but what things soever he shall hear, these shall he speak: and he shall declare unto you the things that are to come. He shall glorify me: for he shall take of mine, and shall declare it unto you. All things whatsoever the Father hath are mine: therefore said I, that he taketh; of mine, and shall declare it unto you. A little while, and ye behold me no more; and again a little while, and ye shall see me."

Some of his disciples therefore said one to another. "What is this that he saith unto us, 'A little while, and ye behold me not; and again a little while, and ye shall see me': and 'Because I go to the Father'?"

They said therefore, "What is this that he saith, 'A little while'? We know not what he saith."

Jesus perceived that they were desirous to ask him, and he said unto them, "Do ye inquire among yourselves concerning this, that I said, 'A little while, and ye behold me not, and again a little while, and ye shall see me?' Verily, verily, I say unto you, that ye shall weep and lament, but the world shall rejoice: ye shall be sorrowful, but your sorrow shall be turned into joy. A woman when she is in travail hath sorrow, because her hour is come: but when she is delivered of the child she remembereth no more the anguish, for the joy that a man is born into the world. And ye therefore now have sorrow: but I will see you again, and your heart shall rejoice, and your joy no one taketh away from you. And in that day ye shall ask me no question. Verily, verily, I say unto you, If ye shall ask anything of the Father, he will give it you in my name. Hitherto have ye asked nothing in my name: ask, and ye shall receive, that your joy may be made full.

"These things have I spoken unto you in dark sayings: the hour cometh, when I shall no more speak unto you in dark sayings, but shall tell you plainly of the Father. In that day ye shall ask in my name: and I say not unto you, that I will pray the Father for you; for the Father himself loveth you, because ye have loved me, and have believed that I came forth from the Father. I came out from the Father, and am come into the world; again, I leave the world, and go unto the Father."

His disciples say, "Lo, now speakest thou plainly, and speakest no dark saying. Now know we that thou knowest all things, and needest not that any man should ask thee: by this we believe that thou camest forth from God."

Jesus answered them, "Do ye now believe? Behold, the hour cometh, yea, is come, that ye shall be scattered, every man to his own, and shall leave me alone: and yet I am not alone, because the Father is with me. These things have I spoken unto you, that in me ye may have peace. In the world ye have tribulation: but be of good cheer: I have overcome the world."

THE INTERCESSORY PRAYER.

These things spake Jesus; and lifting up his eyes to heaven, he said, "Father, the hour is come; glorify thy Son, that the Son may glorify thee: even as thou gavest him authority over all flesh, that to all whom thou hast given him, he should give eternal life. And this is life eternal, that they should know thee the only true God, and him whom thou didst send, even Jesus Christ. I glorified thee on the earth, having accomplished the work which thou hast given me to do. And now, Father, glorify thou me with thine own self with the glory which I had with thee before the world was. I manifested thy name unto the men whom thou gavest me out of the world: thine they were, and thou gavest them to me; and they have kept thy word. Now they know that all things whatsoever thou hast given me are from thee: for the words which thou gavest me I have given unto them; and they received them, and knew of a truth that I came forth from thee, and they believed that thou didst send me. I pray for them: I pray not for the world, but for those whom thou hast given me; for they are thine: and all things that are mine are thine, and thine are mine; and I am glorified in them. And I am no more in the world, and these are in the world, and I come to thee. Holy Father, keep them in thy name which thou hast given me, that they may be one, even as we are. While I was with them, I kept them in thy name which thou hast given me; and I guarded them, and not one of them perished, but the son of perdition; that the scripture might be fulfilled. But now I come to thee; and these things I speak in the world, that they may have my joy made full in themselves. I have given them thy word, and the world hated them, because they are not of the world, even as I am not of the world. I pray not that thou shouldest take them from the world, but that thou shouldst keep them from the evil one. They are not of the world, even as I am not of the world. Sanctify them in the truth: thy word is truth. As thou didst send me into the world, even so sent I them into the world. And for their sakes I sanctify myself, that they themselves also may be sanctified in truth. Neither for these only do I pray, but for them also that believe on me through their word; that they may all be one; even as thou, Father, art in me, and I in thee, that they also may be in us: that the world may believe that thou didst send me. And the glory which thou hast given me I have given unto them; that they may be one, even as we are one; I in them, and thou in me, that they may be perfected into one; that the world may know that thou didst send me, and lovedst them, even as thou lovedst me. Father, I desire that they also whom thou hast given me be with me where I am, that they may behold my glory, which thou hast given me: for thou lovedst me before the foundation of the world. O righteous Father, the world knew thee not, but I knew thee; and these knew that thou didst send me; and I made known unto them thy name, and will make it known; that the love wherewith thou lovedst me may be in them, and I in them."

And when they had sung a hymn, they went out into the mount of Olives.

FRIDAY--THE DAY OF SUFFERING
THE AGONY IN GETHSEMANE.

And they come unto a place which was named Gethsemane: and he saith unto his disciples, "Sit ye here, while I pray."

And he taketh with him Peter and James and John, and began to be greatly amazed, and sore troubled. And he saith unto them, "My soul is exceeding sorrowful, even unto death: abide ye here, and watch."

And he went forward a little, and fell on the ground, and prayed that, if it were possible, the hour might pass away from him.

And he said, "Abba, Father, all things are possible unto thee; remove this cup from me: howbeit not what I will, but what thou wilt."

And there appeared unto him an angel from heaven, strengthening him.

And being in an agony, he prayed more earnestly; and his sweat became as it were great drops of blood falling down upon the ground.

And when he rose up from his prayer, he came unto the disciples, and found them sleeping for sorrow, and said unto Peter, "Simon, sleepest thou? Couldest thou not watch one hour? Watch and pray, that ye enter not into temptation: the spirit indeed is willing, but the flesh is weak."

Again a second time he went away, and prayed, saying, "My Father, if this cannot pass away, except I drink it, thy will be done."

And he came again and found them sleeping, for their eyes were heavy. And he left them again, and went away, and prayed a third time, saying the same words.

Then cometh he to the disciples, and saith unto them, "Sleep on now, and take your rest: behold, the hour is at hand, and the Son of man is betrayed into the hands of sinners.

"Arise, let us be going: behold, he is at hand that betrayeth me."

THE BETRAYAL AND ARREST.

And straightway, while he yet spake, cometh Judas, one of the twelve, and with him a multitude with swords and staves, from the chief priests and the scribes and the elders.

Now he that betrayed him had given them a token, saying, "Whomsoever I shall kiss, that is he; take him, and lead him away safely." And when he was come, straightway he came to him, and saith, "Rabbi," and kissed him.

But Jesus said unto him, "Judas, betrayest thou the Son of man with a kiss?"

Jesus, therefore, knowing all the things that were coming upon him, went forth, and saith unto them. "Whom seek ye?"

They answered him, "Jesus of Nazareth."

Jesus saith unto them. "I am he."

And Judas also, who betrayed him. was standing with them. When therefore he said unto them, "I am he," they went backward, and fell to the ground.

Again therefore he asked them, "Whom seek ye?"

And they said, "Jesus of Nazareth."

Jesus answered, "I told you that I am he; if therefore ye seek me, let these go their way": that the word might be fulfilled which he spake, "Of those whom thou hast given me I lost not one."

And when they that were about him saw what would follow, they said, "Lord, shall we smite with the sword?"

Simon Peter therefore having a sword drew it, and struck the high priest's servant, and cut off his right ear. Now the servant's name was Malchus.

But Jesus answered and said, "Suffer ye them thus far." And he touched his ear, and healed him.

Then saith Jesus unto Peter, "Put up again thy sword into its place: for all they that take the sword shall perish with the sword. Or thinkest thou that I cannot beseech my Father and he shall even now send me more than twelve legions of angels? How then should the scriptures be fulfilled, that thus it must be? The cup which the Father hath given me, shall I not drink it?"

And Jesus said unto the chief priest's and captains of the temple, and elders, that were come against him, "Are ye come out, as against a robber, with swords and staves? When I was daily with you in the temple, ye stretched not forth your hands against me: but this is your hour, and the power of darkness."

Then all the disciples left him, and fled.

And a certain young man followed with him, having a linen cloth cast about him, over his naked body; and they lay hold on him; but he left the linen cloth, and fled naked.

THE TRIAL BEFORE THE JEWISH AUTHORITIES.

So the band and the chief captain, and the officers of the Jews, seized Jesus and bound him, and led him to Annas first; for he was father in law to Caiaphas, who was high priest that year. Now Caiaphas was he that gave counsel to the Jews, that it was expedient that one man should die for the people.

And Simon Peter followed Jesus, and so did another disciple. Now that disciple was known unto the high priest, and entered in with Jesus into the court of the high priest; but Peter was standing at the door without. So the other disciple, who was known unto the high priest, went out and spake unto her that kept the door, and brought in Peter.

The maid therefore that kept the door saith unto Peter, "Art thou also one of this man's disciples?"

He saith, "I am not."

Now the servants and the officers were standing there, having made a fire of coals; for it was cold; and they were warming themselves; and Peter also was with them standing and warming himself.

The high priest therefore asked Jesus of his disciples, and of his teaching. Jesus answered him, "I have spoken openly to the world; I ever taught in synagogues, and in the temple, where all the Jews come together; and in secret spake I nothing. Why askest thou me? Ask them that have heard me, what I spake unto them: behold, these know the things which I said."

And when he had said this, one of the officers standing by struck Jesus with his hand, saying, "Answerest thou the high priest so?"

Jesus answered him, "If I have spoken evil, bear witness of the evil; but if well, why smitest thou me?"

Annas therefore sent him bound unto Caiaphas the high priest.

Now the chief priests and the whole council sought witness against Jesus to put him to death; and found it not. For many bare false witness against him, and their witness agreed not together. And there stood up certain, and bare false witness against him, saying, "We heard him say, I will destroy this temple that is made with hands, and in three days I will build another made without hands." And not even so did their witness agree together.

And the high priest stood up in the midst, and asked Jesus, saying, "Answerest thou nothing? What is it which these witness against thee?"

But he held his peace, and answered nothing.

And the high priest said unto him, "I adjure thee by the living God, that thou tell us whether thou art the Christ, the Son of God."

And Jesus said, "I am: and ye shall see the Son of man sitting at the right hand of Power, and coming with the clouds of heaven."

And the high priest rent his clothes, and saith, "What further need have we of witnesses? Ye have heard the blasphemy: what think ye?"

And they all condemned him to be worthy of death.

Then did they spit in his face and buffet him. And they blindfolded him and smote him with the palms of their hands, saying, "Prophesy unto us, thou Christ: who is he that struck thee?"

THE DENIAL OF PETER.

And as Peter was beneath in the court, there cometh one of the maids of the high priest; and seeing Peter warming himself, she looked upon him, and saith, "Thou also wast with the Nazarene, even Jesus."

But he denied, saying, "I neither know nor understand what thou sayest," and he went out into the porch; and the cock crew.

And after a little while they that stood by came and said to Peter, "Of a truth thou also art one of them; for thy speech maketh thee known."

Then began he to curse and to swear, "I know not the man." And straightway the cock crew.

And the Lord turned, and looked upon Peter. And Peter remembered the word of the Lord, how that he said unto him, "Before the cock crow twice thou shalt deny me thrice."

And he went out, and wept bitterly.

*   *   *   *   *

And straightway in the morning the chief priests with the elders and scribes, and the whole council, held a consultation, and bound Jesus, and carried him away, and delivered him up to Pilate, the governor.

THE REMORSE OF JUDAS.

Then Judas, who betrayed him, when he saw that he was condemned, repented himself, and brought back the thirty pieces of silver to the chief priests and elders, saying, "I have sinned in that I betrayed innocent blood."

But they said, "What is that to us? See thou to it."

And he cast down the pieces of silver into the sanctuary, and departed; and he went away and hanged himself.

And the chief priests took the pieces of silver, and said, "It is not lawful to put them into the treasury, since it is the price of blood." And they took counsel, and bought with them the potter's field, to bury strangers in. Wherefore that field was called, "The field of blood," unto this day.

Then was fulfilled that which was spoken through Jeremiah the prophet, saying, "And they took the thirty pieces of silver, the price of him that was priced, whom certain of the children of Israel did price; and they gave them for the potter's field, as the Lord appointed me."

THE TRIAL BEFORE PILATE.

They lead Jesus therefore from Caiaphas into the Praetorium: and it was early; and they themselves entered not into the Praetorium, that they might not be defiled, but might eat the passover. Pilate therefore went out unto them, and saith, "What accusation bring ye against this man?"

They answered and said unto him, "If this man were not an evil-doer, we should not have delivered him up unto thee."

Pilate therefore said unto them, "Take him yourselves, and judge him according to your law."

The Jews said unto him, "It is not lawful for us to put any man to death": that the word of Jesus might be fulfilled, which he spake, signifying by what manner of death he should die.

And they began to accuse him, saying, "We found this man perverting our nation, and forbidding to give tribute to Caesar, and saying that he himself is Christ a king."

And when he was accused by the chief priests and elders, he answered nothing. Then saith Pilate unto him, "Hearest thou not how many things they witness against thee?" And he gave him no answer, not even to one word: insomuch that the governor marvelled greatly.

Pilate therefore entered again into the Praetorium, and called Jesus, and said unto him, "Art thou the King of the Jews?"

Jesus answered, "Sayest thou this of thyself, or did others tell it thee concerning me?"

Pilate answered, "Am I a Jew? Thine own nation and the chief priests delivered thee unto me: what hast thou done?"

Jesus answered, "My kingdom is not of this world: if my kingdom were of this world, then would my servants fight, that I should not be delivered to the Jews; but now is my kingdom not from hence."

Pilate therefore said unto him, "Art thou a king then?"

Jesus answered, "Thou sayest that I am a king. To this end have I been born, and to this end am I come into the world, that I should bear witness unto the truth. Every one that is of the truth heareth my voice."

Pilate saith unto him, "What is truth?"

And when he had said this, he went out again unto the Jews, and saith unto them, "I find no crime in him."

But they were the more urgent, saying, "He stirreth up the people, teaching throughout all Judaea, and beginning from Galilee, even unto this place."

But when Pilate heard it, he asked whether the man were a Galilaean. And when he knew that he was of Herod's jurisdiction, he sent him unto Herod, who himself also was at Jerusalem in these days.

JESUS BEFORE HEROD.

Now when Herod saw Jesus, he was exceeding glad; for he was of a long time desirous to see him, because he had heard concerning him; and he hoped to see some miracle done by him. And he questioned him in many words; but he answered him nothing. And the chief priests and the scribes stood, vehemently accusing him. And Herod with his soldiers set him at nought, and mocked him, and arraying him in gorgeous apparel sent him back to Pilate.

And Herod and Pilate became friends with each other that very day: for before they were at enmity between themselves.

THE TRIAL BEFORE PILATE RESUMED.

And Pilate called together the chief priests and the rulers and the people, and said unto them, "Ye brought unto me this man, as one that perverteth the people: and behold, I, having examined him before you, found no fault in this man touching those things whereof ye accuse him: no, nor yet Herod: for he sent him back unto us; and behold, nothing worthy of death hath been done by him. I will therefore chastise him, and release him."

Now at the feast the governor was wont to release unto the multitude one prisoner, whom they would. And they had then a notable prisoner, called Barabbas, lying bound with them that had made insurrection, men who in the insurrection had committed murder. And the multitude went up and began to ask him to do as he was wont to do unto them.

And Pilate answered them, saying, "Will ye that I release unto you the King of the Jews?" For he perceived that for envy the chief priests had delivered him up.

Now the chief priests and the elders persuaded the multitudes that they should ask for Barabbas, and destroy Jesus.

But the governor answered and said unto them, "Which of the two will ye that I release unto you?"

And they said, "Barabbas."

Pilate saith unto them, "What then shall I do unto Jesus who is called Christ?"

They all say, "Let him be crucified."

And he said unto them a third time, "Why, what evil hath this man done? I have found no cause of death in him: I will therefore chastise and release him."

Then Pilate therefore took Jesus, and scourged him.

And the soldiers led him away within the court, which is the Praetorium; and they call together the whole band.

And they stripped him, and arrayed him in a purple garment. And they platted a crown of thorns and put it upon his head, and a reed in his right hand; and they kneeled down before him, and mocked him, saying: "Hail, King of the Jews!" and they struck him with their hands. And they spat upon him, and took the reed and smote him upon the head.

And Pilate went out again, and saith unto them, "Behold, I bring him out to you, that ye may know that I find no crime in him."

Jesus therefore came out, wearing the crown of thorns and the purple garment. And Pilate saith unto them, "Behold, the man!"

When therefore the chief priests and the officers saw him, they cried out, saying, "Crucify him, crucify him!"

Pilate saith unto them, "Take him yourselves, and crucify him: for I find no crime in him."

The Jews answered him, "We have a law, and by that law he ought to die, because he made himself the Son of God."

When Pilate therefore heard this saying, he was the more afraid; and he entered into the Praetorium again, and saith unto Jesus, "Whence art thou?"

But Jesus gave him no answer.

Pilate therefore saith unto him, "Speakest thou not unto me? Knowest thou not that I have power to release thee, and have power to crucify thee?"

Jesus answered him, "Thou wouldest have no power against me, except it were given thee from above: therefore he that delivered me unto thee hath greater sin."

Upon this Pilate sought to release him: but the Jews cried out, saying, "If thou release this man, thou art not Caesar's friend: every one that maketh himself a king speaketh against Caesar."

When Pilate therefore heard these words, he brought Jesus out, and sat down on the judgment-seat at a place called The Pavement, but in Hebrew, Gabbatha.

And while he was sitting on the judgment-seat, his wife sent unto him, saying, "Have thou nothing to do with that righteous man; for I have suffered many things this day in a dream because of him."

Now it was the Preparation of the passover: it was about the sixth hour. And he saith unto the Jews, "Behold, your King."

They therefore cried out, "Away with him, away with him, crucify him!"

Pilate saith unto them, "Shall I crucify your King?"

The chief priests answered, "We have no king but Caesar."

So when Pilate saw that he prevailed nothing, but rather that a tumult was arising, he took water, and washed his hands before the multitude, saying, "I am innocent of the blood of this righteous man; see ye to it."

And all the people answered and said, "His blood be on us, and on our children."

And they were urgent with loud voices asking that he might be crucified. And their voices prevailed.

And Pilate, wishing to content the multitude, gave sentence that what they asked for should be done. And he released unto them Barabbas, him that for insurrection and murder had been cast into prison, whom they asked for; but Jesus he delivered up to their will.

And when they had mocked him, they took off from him the robe, and put on him his garments, and led him away to crucify him.

THE SORROWFUL WAY.

They took Jesus therefore: and he went out, bearing the cross for himself.

And as they came out, they laid hold upon one Simon of Cyrene, the father of Alexander and Rufus, who was passing by, coming from the country; him they compelled to go with them, and laid on him the cross, that he might bear it after Jesus.

And there followed him a great multitude of the people, and of women who bewailed and lamented him.

But Jesus turning unto them said, "Daughters of Jerusalem, weep not for me, but weep for yourselves, and for your children. For behold, the days are coming, in which they shall say, 'Blessed are the barren, and the wombs that never bare, and the breasts that never gave suck.' Then shall they begin to say to the mountains, 'Fall on us;' and to the hills, 'Cover us.' For if they do these things in the green tree, what shall be done in the dry?"

And there were also two others, malefactors, led with him to be put to death.

THE CRUCIFIXION.

And when they were come unto a place called Golgotha, that is to say, The place of a skull, they gave him wine to drink mingled with gall: and when he had tasted it, he would not drink.

There they crucified him, and the malefactors, one on the right hand and the other on the left.

And Jesus said, "Father, forgive them; for they know not what they do."

And Pilate wrote a title also, and put it on the cross. And there was written:

JESUS OF NAZARETH, THE KING OF THE JEWS.

This title therefore read many of the Jews, for the place where Jesus was crucified was nigh to the city; and it was written in Hebrew, and in Latin, and in Greek.

The chief priests of the Jews therefore said to Pilate, "Write not, 'The King of the Jews,' but that he said, 'I am King of the Jews.'"

Pilate answered, "What I have written I have written."

The soldiers therefore, when they had crucified Jesus, took his garments and made four parts, to every soldier a part; and also the coat: now the coat was without seam, woven from the top throughout. They said therefore one to another, "Let us not rend it, but cast lots for it, whose it shall be": that the scripture might be fulfilled, which saith,

"They parted my garments among them,
And upon my vesture did they cast lots."

These things therefore the soldiers did; and they sat and watched him there.

And the people stood beholding.

And they that passed by railed on him, wagging their heads, and saying, "Thou that destroyest the temple, and buildest it in three days, save thyself: if thou art the Son of God, come down from the cross."

In like manner also, the chief priests mocking him, with the scribes and elders, said, "He saved others; himself he cannot save. Let the Christ, the King of Israel, now come down from the cross, that we may see and believe. He trusteth on God; let him deliver him now, if he desireth him: for he said, I am the Son of God."

And one of the malefactors that were hanged railed on him, saying, "Art not thou the Christ? Save thyself and us."

But the other answered, and rebuking him said, "Dost thou not even fear God, seeing thou art in the same condemnation? And we indeed justly; for we receive the due reward of our deeds: but this man hath done nothing amiss." And he said, "Jesus, remember me when thou comest in thy kingdom."

And he said unto him, "Verily I say unto thee, To-day shalt thou be with me in Paradise."

But there were standing by the cross of Jesus his mother, and his mother's sister, Mary the wife of Clopas, and Mary Magdalene. When Jesus therefore saw his mother, and the disciple standing by whom he loved, he saith unto his mother, "Woman, behold thy son!"

Then saith he to the disciple, "Behold, thy mother!"

And from that hour the disciple took her unto his own home.

And when the sixth hour was come, there was darkness over the whole land until the ninth hour. And at the ninth hour Jesus cried with a loud voice, "Eloi, Eloi, lama sabachthani?" which is, being interpreted. "My God, my God, why hast thou forsaken me."

And some of them that stood by, when they heard it, said, "Behold, he calleth Elijah."

After this, Jesus, knowing that all things are now finished, that the scripture might be accomplished, saith, "I thirst."

There was set there a vessel full of vinegar: so they put a sponge full of the vinegar upon hyssop, and brought it to his mouth. When Jesus therefore had received the vinegar, he said, "It is finished."

And Jesus, crying with a loud voice, said, "Father, into thy hands I commend my spirit," and having said this, he gave up the ghost.

And behold, the veil of the temple was rent in two from the top to the bottom; and the earth did quake; and the rocks were rent; and the tombs were opened; and many bodies of the saints that had fallen asleep were raised; and coming forth out of the tombs after his resurrection they entered into the holy city and appeared unto many.

Now the centurion, and they that were with him watching Jesus, when they saw the earthquake, and the things that were done, feared exceedingly, saying, "Truly this was the Son of God."

And all the multitudes that came together to this sight, when they beheld the things that were done, returned smiting their breasts. And many women were there beholding from afar, who had followed Jesus from Galilee, ministering unto him; among whom was Mary Magdalene, and Mary the mother of James and Joses, and the mother of the sons of Zebedee.

The Jews therefore, because it was the Preparation, that the bodies should not remain on the cross upon the sabbath (for the day of that sabbath was a high day), asked of Pilate that their legs might be broken and that they might be taken away.

The soldiers therefore came, and brake the legs of the first, and of the other that was crucified with him: but when they came to Jesus, and saw that he was dead already, they brake not his legs: howbeit one of the soldiers with a spear pierced his side, and straightway there came out blood and water. And he that hath seen hath borne witness, and his witness is true: and he knoweth that he saith true, that ye also may believe. For these things came to pass, that the scripture might be fulfilled, "A bone of him shall not be broken." And again another scripture saith, "They shall look on him whom they pierced."

THE BURIAL.

And after these things, when even was come, there came a rich man from Arimathaea, named Joseph, a councillor of honorable estate, a disciple of Jesus, but secretly for fear of the Jews; and he boldly went in unto Pilate and asked for the body of Jesus. And Pilate marvelled if he were already dead: and calling unto him the centurion, he asked him whether he had been any while dead. And when he learned it of the centurion, he granted the corpse to Joseph.

He came therefore, and took away his body. And there came also Nicodemus, he who at the first came to him by night, bringing a mixture of myrrh and aloes, about a hundred pounds. So they took the body of Jesus, and bound it in linen cloths with the spices, as the custom of the Jews is to bury.

Now in the place where he was crucified there was a garden: and in the garden a new tomb wherein was never man yet laid. There then because of the Jews' Preparation (for the tomb was nigh at hand), they laid Jesus; and rolled a stone against the door of the tomb.

And Mary Magdalene and Mary the mother of Jesus beheld the tomb, and how his body was laid. And they returned, and prepared spices and ointments.

SATURDAY--THE DAY OF SILENCE AND SOR-ROW
THE WATCH AT THE TOMB.

Now on the morrow, which is the day after the Preparation, the chief priests and the Pharisees were gathered together unto Pilate, saying, "Sir, we remember that that deceiver said while he was yet alive, 'After three days I rise again.' Command therefore that the sepulchre be made sure until the third day, lest haply his disciples come and steal him away, and say unto the people, 'He is risen from the dead,' and the last error will be worse than the first."

Pilate said unto them, "Ye have a guard: go, make it as sure as ye can."

So they went, and made the sepulchre sure, sealing the stone, the guard being with them.

=HIS RESURRECTION=

SUNDAY--THE DAY OF RESURRECTION
THE EARTHQUAKE.

And behold, there was a great earthquake; for an angel of the Lord descended from heaven, and came and rolled away the stone, and sat upon it. His appearance was as lightning, and his raiment white as snow: and for fear of him the watchers did quake, and became as dead men.

THE EMPTY TOMB.

Now on the first day of the week cometh Mary Magdalene early, while it was yet dark, unto the tomb, and seeth the stone taken away from the tomb. She runneth therefore, and cometh to Simon Peter, and to the other disciple whom Jesus loved, and saith unto them, "They have taken away the Lord out of the tomb, and we know not where they have laid him."

Peter therefore went forth, and the other disciple, and they went toward the tomb. And they ran both together: and the other disciple outran Peter, and came first to the tomb; and stooping and looking in, he seeth the linen cloths lying; yet entered he not in.

Simon Peter therefore also cometh, following him, and entered into the tomb; and he beholdeth the linen cloths lying, and the napkin, that was upon his head, not lying with the linen cloths, but rolled up in a place by itself. Then entered in therefore the other disciple also, who came first to the tomb, and he saw, and believed. For as yet they knew not the scripture, that he must rise again from the dead. So the disciples went away again unto their own home.

THE APPEARANCE TO MARY.

But Mary was standing without at the tomb weeping: so, as she wept, she stooped and looked into the tomb; and she beholdeth two angels in white sitting, one at the head, and one at the feet, where the body of Jesus had lain. And they say unto her, "Woman, why weepest thou?"

She saith unto them, "Because they have taken away my Lord, and I know not where they have laid him."

When she had thus said, she turned herself back, and beholdeth Jesus standing, and knew not that it was Jesus.

Jesus saith unto her, "Woman, why weepest thou? Whom seekest thou?"

She, supposing him to be the gardener, saith unto him, "Sir, if thou hast borne him hence, tell me where thou hast laid him, and I will take him away."

Jesus saith unto her, "Mary."

She turneth herself, and saith unto him in Hebrew, "Rabboni"; which is to say, "Teacher."

Jesus saith to her, "Touch me not; for I am not yet ascended unto the Father: but go unto my brethren, and say to them, 'I ascend unto my Father, and your Father, and my God and your God.'"

Mary Magdalene cometh and telleth the disciples, "I have seen the Lord"; and that he had said these things unto her.

THE APPEARANCE TO THE WOMEN.

And the women which had come with him out of Galilee came unto the tomb, bringing the spices which they had prepared. And they were saying among themselves, "Who shall roll us away the stone from the door of the tomb?" and looking up, they see that the stone is rolled back: for it was exceeding great. And entering into the tomb, they saw a young man sitting on the right side arrayed in a white robe; and they were amazed. And he saith unto them, "Be not amazed: ye seek Jesus, the Nazarene, who hath been crucified: he is risen; he is not here: behold, the place where they laid him! But go, tell his disciples and Peter, 'He goeth before you into Galilee: there shall ye see him, as he said unto you.'"

And they departed quickly from the tomb with fear and great joy, and ran to bring his disciples word.

And behold, Jesus met them, saying, "All hail." And they came and took hold of his feet, and worshipped him.

Then saith Jesus unto them, "Fear not: go tell my brethren that they depart into Galilee, and there shall they see me."

REPORT OF THE WATCH.

Now while they were going, behold, some of the guard came into the city, and told unto the chief priests all the things that were come to pass. And when they were assembled with the elders, and had taken counsel, they gave much money unto the soldiers, saying, "Say ye, 'His disciples came by night, and stole him away while we slept.' And if this come to the governor's ears, we will persuade him, and rid you of care."

So they took the money and did as they were taught: and this saying was spread abroad among the Jews, and continueth until this day.

THE APPEARANCE AT EMMAUS.

And behold, two of them were going that very day to a village named Emmaus, which was three-score furlongs from Jerusalem. And they communed with each other of all these things which had happened.

And it came to pass, while they communed and questioned together, that Jesus himself drew near, and went with them. But their eyes were holden that they should not know him.

And he said unto them, "What communications are these that ye have one with another, as ye walk?"

And they stood still, looking sad. And one of them, named Cleopas, answering, said unto him, "Dost thou alone sojourn in Jerusalem and not know the things which are come to pass there in these days?'"

And he said unto them, "What things?"

And they said unto him, "The things concerning Jesus the Nazarene, who was a prophet mighty in deed and word before God, and all the people: and how the chief priests and our rulers delivered him up to be condemned to death, and crucified him. But we hoped that it was he who should redeem Israel. Yea, and besides all this, it is now the third day since these things came to pass. Moreover, certain women of our company amazed us, having been early at the tomb; and when they found not his body, they came, saying, that they had also seen a vision of angels, who said that he was alive. And certain of them that were with us went to the tomb, and found it even so as the women had said: but him they saw not."

And he said unto them, "O foolish men, and slow of heart to believe in all that the prophets have spoken! Behooved it not the Christ to suffer these things, and to enter into his glory?"

And beginning from Moses and from all the prophets, he interpreted to them in all the scriptures the things concerning himself.

And they drew nigh unto the village, whither they were going: and he made as though he would go further. And they constrained him, saying, "Abide with us; for it is toward evening, and the day is now far spent."

And he went in to abide with them. And it came to pass, when he had sat down with them to meat, he took the bread and blessed; and breaking it, he gave to them. And their eyes were opened, and they knew him; and he vanished out of their sight.

And they said one to another, "Was not our heart burning within us, while he spake to us in the way, while he opened to us the scriptures?"

And they rose up that very hour, and returned to Jerusalem, and found the eleven gathered together, and them that were with them, saying, "The Lord is risen indeed, and hath appeared to Simon." And they rehearsed the things that happened in the way, and how he was known of them in the breaking of the bread.

THE APPEARANCE TO THE DISCIPLES.

When therefore it was evening, on that day, the first day of the week, and when the doors were shut where the disciples were, for fear of the Jews, Jesus came and stood in the midst and saith unto them, "Peace be unto you."

But they were terrified and affrighted, and supposed that they beheld a spirit. And he said unto them, "Why are ye troubled? and wherefore do questionings arise in your heart? See my hands and my feet, that it is I myself: handle me, and see; for a spirit hath not flesh and bones, as ye behold me having."

And when he had said this, he showed them his hands and his feet.

And while they still disbelieved for joy, and wondered, he said unto them, "Have ye here anything to eat?"

And they gave him a piece of a broiled fish. And he took it, and ate before them.

Jesus therefore said to them again, "Peace be unto you: as the Father hath sent me, even so send I you." And when he had said this, he breathed on them, and saith unto them, "Receive ye the Holy Spirit: whose soever sins ye forgive, they are forgiven unto them; whose soever sins ye retain, they are retained."

AFTER THE RESURRECTION DAY THE APPEARANCE TO THE DISCIPLES AND TO THOMAS.

But Thomas, one of the twelve, called Didymus, was not with them when Jesus came. The other disciples therefore said unto him, "We have seen the Lord."

But he said unto them, "Except I shall see in his hands the print of the nails, and put my finger into the print of the nails, and put my hand into his side, I will not believe."

And after eight days again his disciples were within, and Thomas with them.

Jesus cometh, the doors being shut, and stood in the midst, and said, "Peace be unto you."

Then saith he to Thomas, "Reach hither thy finger, and see my hands; and reach hither thy hand, and put it into my side: and be not faithless, but believing."

Thomas answered and said unto him, "My Lord and my God."

Jesus saith unto him, "Because thou hast seen me, thou hast believed: blessed are they that have not seen, and yet have believed."

THE APPEARANCE TO THE SEVEN BY THE SEA.

After these things Jesus manifested himself again to the disciples at the sea of Tiberias; and he manifested himself on this wise. There were together Simon Peter, and Thomas called Didymus and Nathanael of Cana in Galilee, and the sons of Zebedee, and two other of his disciples.

Simon Peter saith unto them, "I go a fishing."

They say unto him, "We also come with thee."

They went forth, and entered into the boat; and that night they took nothing. But when day was now breaking, Jesus stood on the beach: yet the disciples knew not that it was Jesus.

Jesus therefore saith unto them, "Children, have ye aught to eat?"

They answered him, "No."

And he said unto them, "Cast the net on the right side of the boat, and ye shall find."

They cast therefore, and now they were not able to draw it for the multitude of fishes.

That disciple therefore whom Jesus loved saith unto Peter, "It is the Lord". So when Simon Peter heard that it was the Lord, he girt his coat about him (for he was naked), and cast himself into the sea.

But the other disciples came in the little boat (for they were not far from the land, but about two hundred cubits off), dragging the net full of fishes.

So when they got out upon the land, they see a fire of coals there, and fish laid thereon, and bread. Jesus saith unto them, "Bring of the fish which ye have now taken."

Simon Peter therefore went up, and drew the net to land, full of great fishes, a hundred and fifty and three; and for all there were so many, the net was not rent.

Jesus saith unto them, "Come and break your fast."

And none of the disciples durst inquire of him, "Who art thou?" knowing that it was the Lord.

Jesus cometh, and taketh the bread, and giveth them, and the fish likewise.

This is now the third time that Jesus was manifested to the disciples, after that he was risen from the dead.

So when they had broken their fast, Jesus saith to Simon Peter, "Simon, son of John, lovest thou me more than these?"

He saith unto him, "Yea, Lord; thou knowest that I love thee."

He saith unto him, "Feed my lambs."

He saith unto him again a second time, "Simon, son of John, lovest thou me?"

He saith unto him, "Yea, Lord, thou knowest that I love thee."

He saith unto him, "Tend my sheep."

He saith unto him the third time, "Simon, son of John, lovest thou me?"

Peter was grieved because he said unto him the third time, "Lovest thou me?" And he said unto him, "Lord, thou knowest all things; thou knowest that I love thee."

Jesus saith unto him, "Feed my sheep. Verily, verily, I say unto thee, When thou wast young, thou girdedst thyself, and walkedst whither thou wouldest; but when thou shalt be old, thou shalt stretch forth thy hands, and another shall gird thee, and carry thee whither thou wouldest not."

Now this he spake, signifying by what manner of death he should glorify God. And when he had spoken this, he saith unto him, "Follow me."

Peter, turning about, seeth the disciple whom Jesus loved following; who also leaned back on his breast at the supper, and said, "Lord, who is he that betrayeth thee?" Peter therefore seeing him saith to Jesus, "Lord, and what shall this man do?"

Jesus saith unto him, "If I will that he tarry till I come, what is that to thee? Follow thou me."

This saying therefore went forth among the brethren, that that disciple should not die: yet Jesus said not unto him, that he should not die, but, "If I will that he tarry till I come, what is that to thee?"

THE APPEARANCE TO THE ELEVEN ON THE MOUNTAIN.

The eleven disciples went into Galilee, unto the mountain where Jesus had appointed them. And when they saw him, they worshipped him; but some doubted. And Jesus came to them and spake unto them, saying, "All authority hath been given unto me in heaven and on earth. Go ye therefore, and make disciples of all the nations, baptizing them in the name of the Father and of the Son and of the Holy Spirit: teaching them to observe all things whatsoever I commanded you: and lo, I am with you always, even unto the end of the world."

THE LAST APPEARANCE AND ASCENSION.

And he said unto them, "These are my words which I spake unto you, while I was yet with you, that all things must needs be fulfilled, which are written in the law of Moses, and the prophets, and the psalms, concerning me."

Then opened he their mind, that they might understand the scriptures; and he said unto them, "Thus it is written, that the Christ should suffer, and rise again from the dead the third day; and that repentance and remission of sins should be preached in his name unto all the nations, beginning from Jerusalem. Ye are witnesses of these things. And behold, I send forth the promise of my Father upon you: but tarry ye in the city, until ye be clothed with power from on high."

And he led them out until they were over against Bethany: and he lifted up his hands, and blessed them.

And it came to pass, while he blessed them, he parted from them, and was carried up into heaven. And they worshipped him, and returned to Jerusalem with great joy: and were continually in the temple, blessing God.

*   *   *   *   *

MANY OTHER SIGNS THEREFORE DID JESUS IN THE PRESENCE OF THE DISCIPLES WHICH ARE NOT WRITTEN IN THIS BOOK, BUT THESE ARE WRITTEN, THAT YE MAY BELIEVE THAT JESUS IS THE CHRIST, THE SON OF GOD; AND THAT BELIEVING YE MAY HAVE LIFE IN HIS NAME.

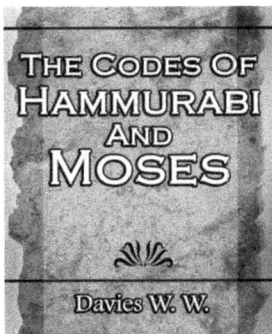

The Codes Of Hammurabi And Moses
W. W. Davies

QTY

The discovery of the Hammurabi Code is one of the greatest achievements of archaeology, and is of paramount interest, not only to the student of the Bible, but also to all those interested in ancient history...

Religion   **ISBN:** *1-59462-338-4*   **Pages:132**
MSRP $12.95

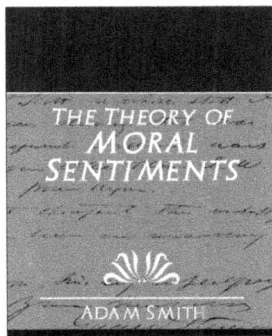

The Theory of Moral Sentiments
Adam Smith

QTY

This work from 1749. contains original theories of conscience amd moral judgment and it is the foundation for systemof morals.

Philosophy   **ISBN:** *1-59462-777-0*   **Pages:536**
MSRP $19.95

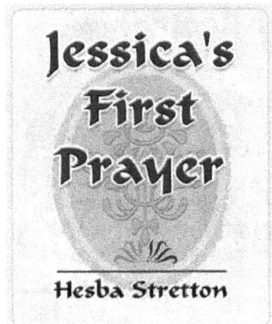

Jessica's First Prayer
Hesba Stretton

QTY

In a screened and secluded corner of one of the many railway-bridges which span the streets of London there could be seen a few years ago, from five o'clock every morning until half past eight, a tidily set-out coffee-stall, consisting of a trestle and board, upon which stood two large tin cans, with a small fire of charcoal burning under each so as to keep the coffee boiling during the early hours of the morning when the work-people were thronging into the city on their way to their daily toil...

Childrens   **ISBN:** *1-59462-373-2*   **Pages:84**
MSRP $9.95

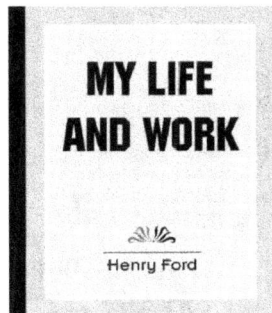

My Life and Work
Henry Ford

QTY

Henry Ford revolutionized the world with his implementation of mass production for the Model T automobile. Gain valuable business insight into his life and work with his own auto-biography... "We have only started on our development of our country we have not as yet, with all our talk of wonderful progress, done more than scratch the surface. The progress has been wonderful enough out..."

Biographies/ **ISBN:** *1-59462-198-5*   **Pages:300**
MSRP $21.95

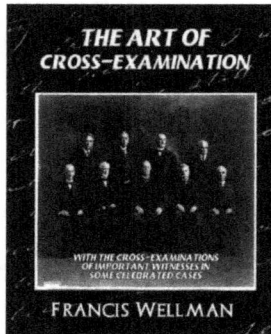

The Art of Cross-Examination
Francis Wellman

QTY

I presume it is the experience of every author, after his first book is published upon an important subject, to be almost overwhelmed with a wealth of ideas and illustrations which could readily have been included in his book, and which to his own mind, at least, seem to make a second edition inevitable. Such certainly was the case with me; and when the first edition had reached its sixth impression in five months, I rejoiced to learn that it seemed to my publishers that the book had met with a sufficiently favorable reception to justify a second and considerably enlarged edition. ..

Pages:412

Reference   ISBN: *1-59462-647-2*   *MSRP $19.95*

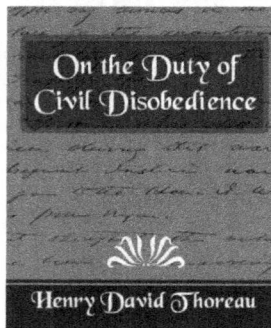

On the Duty of Civil Disobedience
Henry David Thoreau

QTY

Thoreau wrote his famous essay, On the Duty of Civil Disobedience, as a protest against an unjust but popular war and the immoral but popular institution of slave-owning. He did more than write—he declined to pay his taxes, and was hauled off to gaol in consequence. Who can say how much this refusal of his hastened the end of the war and of slavery ?

Law   ISBN: *1-59462-747-9*   **Pages:48**

MSRP $7.45

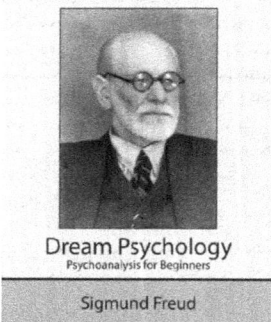

Dream Psychology Psychoanalysis for Beginners
Sigmund Freud

QTY

Sigmund Freud, born Sigismund Schlomo Freud (May 6, 1856 - September 23, 1939), was a Jewish-Austrian neurologist and psychiatrist who co-founded the psychoanalytic school of psychology. Freud is best known for his theories of the unconscious mind, especially involving the mechanism of repression; his redefinition of sexual desire as mobile and directed towards a wide variety of objects; and his therapeutic techniques, especially his understanding of transference in the therapeutic relationship and the presumed value of dreams as sources of insight into unconscious desires.

Pages:196

Psychology   ISBN: *1-59462-905-6*   *MSRP $15.45*

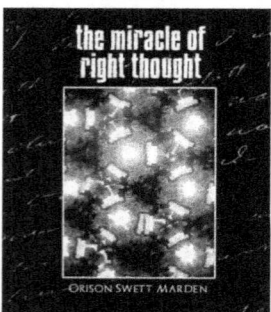

The Miracle of Right Thought
Orison Swett Marden

QTY

Believe with all of your heart that you will do what you were made to do. When the mind has once formed the habit of holding cheerful, happy, prosperous pictures, it will not be easy to form the opposite habit. It does not matter how improbable or how far away this realization may see, or how dark the prospects may be, if we visualize them as best we can, as vividly as possible, hold tenaciously to them and vigorously struggle to attain them, they will gradually become actualized, realized in the life. But a desire, a longing without endeavor, a yearning abandoned or held indifferently will vanish without realization.

Pages:360

Self Help   ISBN: *1-59462-644-8*   *MSRP $25.45*

QTY

☐ **The Rosicrucian Cosmo-Conception Mystic Christianity** *by Max Heindel*　ISBN: *1-59462-188-8*　**$38.95**
The Rosicrucian Cosmo-conception is not dogmatic, neither does it appeal to any other authority than the reason of the student. It is: not controversial, but is: sent forth in the, hope that it may help to clear...　New Age/Religion Pages 646

☐ **Abandonment To Divine Providence** *by Jean-Pierre de Caussade*　ISBN: *1-59462-228-0*　**$25.95**
"The Rev. Jean Pierre de Caussade was one of the most remarkable spiritual writers of the Society of Jesus in France in the 18th Century. His death took place at Toulouse in 1751. His works have gone through many editions and have been republished...　Inspirational/Religion Pages 400

☐ **Mental Chemistry** *by Charles Haanel*　ISBN: *1-59462-192-6*　**$23.95**
Mental Chemistry allows the change of material conditions by combining and appropriately utilizing the power of the mind. Much like applied chemistry creates something new and unique out of careful combinations of chemicals the mastery of mental chemistry...　New Age/Business Pages 354

☐ **The Letters of Robert Browning and Elizabeth Barret Barrett 1845-1846 vol II**　ISBN: *1-59462-193-4*　**$35.95**
by Robert Browning and Elizabeth Barrett　Biographies Pages 596

☐ **Gleanings In Genesis (volume I)** *by Arthur W. Pink*　ISBN: *1-59462-130-6*　**$27.45**
Appropriately has Genesis been termed "the seed plot of the Bible" for in t we have, in germ form, almost all of the great doctrines which are afterwards fully developed in the books of Scripture which follow...　Religion/Inspirational Pages 420

☐ **The Master Key** *by L. W. de Laurence*　ISBN: *1-59462-001-6*　**$30.95**
In no branch of human knowledge has there been a more lively increase of the spirit of research during the past few years than in the study of Psychology, Concentration and Mental Discipline. The requests for authentic lessons in Thought Control, Mental Discipline and...　New Age/Business Pages 422

☐ **The Lesser Key Of Solomon Goetia** *by L. W. de Laurence*　ISBN: *1-59462-092-X*　**$9.95**
This translation of the first book of the "Lemegton" which is now for the first time made accessible to students of Talismanic Magic was done, after careful collation and edition, from numerous Ancient Manuscripts in Hebrew, Latin, and French...　New Age/Occult Pages 92

☐ **Rubaiyat Of Omar Khayyam** *by Edward Fitzgerald*　ISBN: *1-59462-332-5*　**$13.95**
Edward Fitzgerald, whom the world has already learned, in spite of his own efforts to remain within the shadow of anonymity, to look upon as one of the rarest poets of the century, was born at Bredfield, in Suffolk, on the 31st of March, 1809. He was the third son of John Purcell...　Music Pages 172

☐ **Ancient Law** *by Henry Maine*　ISBN: *1-59462-128-4*　**$29.95**
The chief object of the following pages is to indicate some of the earliest ideas of mankind, as they are reflected in Ancient Law, and to point out the relation of those ideas to modern thought.　Religion/History Pages 452

☐ **Far-Away Stories** *by William J. Locke*　ISBN: *1-59462-129-2*　**$19.45**
"Good wine needs no bush, but a collection of mixed vintages does. And this book is just such a collection. Some of the stories I do not want to remain buried for ever in the museum files of dead magazine-numbers an author's not unpardonable vanity..."　Fiction Pages 272

☐ **Life of David Crockett** *by David Crockett*　ISBN: *1-59462-250-7*　**$27.45**
"Colonel David Crockett was one of the most remarkable men of the times in which he lived. Born in humble life, but gifted with a strong will, an indomitable courage, and unremitting perseverance...　Biographies/New Age Pages 424

☐ **Lip-Reading** *by Edward Nitchie*　ISBN: *1-59462-206-X*　**$25.95**
Edward B. Nitchie, founder of the New York School for the Hard of Hearing, now the Nitchie School of Lip-Reading, Inc, wrote "LIP-READING Principles and Practice'. The development and perfecting of this meritorious work on lip-reading was an undertaking...　How-to Pages 400

☐ **A Handbook of Suggestive Therapeutics, Applied Hypnotism, Psychic Science**　ISBN: *1-59462-214-0*　**$24.95**
by Henry Munro　Health/New Age/Health/Self-help Pages 376

☐ **A Doll's House: and Two Other Plays** *by Henrik Ibsen*　ISBN: *1-59462-112-8*　**$19.95**
Henrik Ibsen created this classic when in revolutionary 1848 Rome. Introducing some striking concepts in playwriting for the realist genre, this play has been studied the world over.　Fiction/Classics/Plays 308

☐ **The Light of Asia** *by sir Edwin Arnold*　ISBN: *1-59462-204-3*　**$13.95**
In this poetic masterpiece, Edwin Arnold describes the life and teachings of Buddha. The man who was to become known as Buddha to the world was born as Prince Gautama of India but he rejected the worldly riches and abandoned the reigns of power when...　Religion/History/Biographies Pages 170

☐ **The Complete Works of Guy de Maupassant** *by Guy de Maupassant*　ISBN: *1-59462-157-8*　**$16.95**
"For days and days, nights and nights, I had dreamed of that first kiss which was to consecrate our engagement, and I knew not on what spot I should put my lips..."　Fiction/Classics Pages 240

☐ **The Art of Cross-Examination** *by Francis L. Wellman*　ISBN: *1-59462-309-0*　**$26.95**
Written by a renowned trial lawyer, Wellman imparts his experience and uses case studies to explain how to use psychology to extract desired information through questioning.　How-to/Science/Reference Pages 408

☐ **Answered or Unanswered?** *by Louisa Vaughan*　ISBN: *1-59462-248-5*　**$10.95**
Miracles of Faith in China　Religion Pages 112

☐ **The Edinburgh Lectures on Mental Science (1909)** *by Thomas*　ISBN: *1-59462-008-3*　**$11.95**
This book contains the substance of a course of lectures recently given by the writer in the Queen Street Hall, Edinburgh. Its purpose is to indicate the Natural Principles governing the relation between Mental Action and Material Conditions...　New Age/Psychology Pages 148

☐ **Ayesha** *by H. Rider Haggard*　ISBN: *1-59462-301-5*　**$24.95**
Verily and indeed it is the unexpected that happens! Probably if there was one person upon the earth from whom the Editor of this, and of a certain previous history, did not expect to hear again...　Classics Pages 380

☐ **Ayala's Angel** *by Anthony Trollope*　ISBN: *1-59462-352-X*　**$29.95**
The two girls were both pretty; but Lucy who was twenty-one who supposed to be simple and comparatively unattractive, whereas Ayala was credited, as her Bomswhat romantic name might show, with poetic charm and a taste for romance. Ayala when her father died was nineteen...　Fiction Pages 484

☐ **The American Commonwealth** *by James Bryce*　ISBN: *1-59462-286-8*　**$34.45**
An interpretation of American democratic political theory. It examines political mechanics and society from the perspective of Scotsman James Bryce　Politics Pages 572

☐ **Stories of the Pilgrims** *by Margaret P. Pumphrey*　ISBN: *1-59462-116-0*　**$17.95**
This book explores pilgrims religious oppression in England as well as their escape to Holland and eventual crossing to America on the Mayflower, and their early days in New England...　History Pages 268

QTY

The Fasting Cure *by Sinclair Upton* ISBN: *1-59462-222-1* **$13.95**
In the Cosmopolitan Magazine for May, 1910, and in the Contemporary Review (London) for April, 1910, I published an article dealing with my experiences in fasting. I have written a great many magazine articles, but never one which attracted so much attention... New Age/Self Help/Health Pages 164

Hebrew Astrology *by Sepharial* ISBN: *1-59462-308-2* **$13.45**
In these days of advanced thinking it is a matter of common observation that we have left many of the old landmarks behind and that we are now pressing forward to greater heights and to a wider horizon than that which represented the mind-content of our progenitors... Astrology Pages 144

Thought Vibration or The Law of Attraction in the Thought World ISBN: *1-59462-127-6* **$12.95**
by William Walker Atkinson Psychology/Religion Pages 144

Optimism *by Helen Keller* ISBN: *1-59462-108-X* **$15.95**
Helen Keller was blind, deaf, and mute since 19 months old, yet famously learned how to overcome these handicaps, communicate with the world, and spread her lectures promoting optimism. An inspiring read for everyone... Biographies/Inspirational Pages 84

Sara Crewe *by Frances Burnett* ISBN: *1-59462-360-0* **$9.45**
In the first place, Miss Minchin lived in London. Her home was a large, dull, tall one, in a large, dull square, where all the houses were alike, and all the sparrows were alike, and where all the door-knockers made the same heavy sound... Childrens/Classic Pages 88

The Autobiography of Benjamin Franklin *by Benjamin Franklin* ISBN: *1-59462-135-7* **$24.95**
The Autobiography of Benjamin Franklin has probably been more extensively read than any other American historical work, and no other book of its kind has had such ups and downs of fortune. Franklin lived for many years in England, where he was agent... Biographies/History Pages 332

Name	
Email	
Telephone	
Address	
City, State ZIP	

☐ **Credit Card**   ☐ **Check / Money Order**

Credit Card Number	
Expiration Date	
Signature	

Please Mail to: Book Jungle
PO Box 2226
Champaign, IL 61825
or Fax to: 630-214-0564

ORDERING INFORMATION
web: *www.bookjungle.com*
email: *sales@bookjungle.com*
fax: *630-214-0564*
mail: *Book Jungle PO Box 2226 Champaign, IL 61825*
or PayPal *to sales@bookjungle.com*

Please contact us for bulk discounts

DIRECT-ORDER TERMS

**20% Discount if You Order
Two or More Books**
Free Domestic Shipping!
Accepted: Master Card, Visa,
Discover, American Express

www.ingramcontent.com/pod-product-compliance
Lightning Source LLC
Chambersburg PA
CBHW080506110426
42742CB00017B/3009